THE
MONASTIC
HEART

THE
MONASTIC
HEART

50 Simple Practices for a
Contemplative and Fulfilling Life

~

JOAN CHITTISTER

CONVERGENT
NEW YORK

Published in the United States by Convergent Books, an imprint of
Random House, a division of Penguin Random House LLC, New York.

CONVERGENT BOOKS is a registered trademark and its C colophon
is a trademark of Penguin Random House LLC.

LIBRARY OF CONGRESS CATALOGING-IN-PUBLICATION DATA
Names: Chittister, Joan, author.
Title: The monastic heart / Sister Joan Chittister.
Description: First edition. | New York: Convergent, [2021]
Identifiers: LCCN 2021012932 (print) | LCCN 2021012933 (ebook) |
ISBN 9780593239407 (hardcover) | ISBN 9780593239414 (ebook)
Subjects: LCSH: Benedictines—Spiritual life. | Benedict, Saint, Abbot of Monte
Cassino. Regula. | Monastic and religious life. | Spiritual life—Catholic Church.
Classification: LCC BX3003 .C45 2021 (print) | LCC BX3003 (ebook) |
DDC 248.8/943—dc23
LC record available at https://lccn.loc.gov/2021012932
LC ebook record available at https://lccn.loc.gov/2021012933

Printed in Canada on acid-free paper

crownpublishing.com

2 4 6 8 9 7 5 3 1

First Edition

Title-page image: copyright © iStock.com / SanerG

Book design by Victoria Wong

It is with deep gratitude and long-lived love that I dedicate this book to Mary Lou Kownacki, OSB— whose life inspired this work, whose deep friendship and holy vision have been to me a star, a path, and a prod to the words in my heart.

Contents

Introduction

I am writing this book at a time when the country and the world have just witnessed the frailty of contemporary society and, at the same time, the endurance of the human spirit. Shaken off our social foundations by a global calamity, an invisible virus we could not see coming, we each found ourselves at the end of certainty and the beginning of faith. Where do we go now as individuals to find our way out of the shadows and toward a new light?

The challenge is to determine what is being asked of the human spirit when the pressures of the time seem insoluble and our inherent energy begins to fray. What internal resources can we rely on then if we are ever to become the fullness of ourselves again. It is time to remember what it means to go on when going on is all we can do. It's time to discover what it takes to nourish the vein of tenacity that change requires as it reshapes the systems around us and to face having to cultivate a future we did not seek or imagine.

In every beating heart is a silent undercurrent that calls each of us to the more of ourselves. Like a magnet it draws a person to a place unknown, to the vision of a wiser life, to the desire to become what I feel I must be—but cannot name. The truth is that this deeper part of everyone does not simply develop in us like wild grass. It needs to be cultivated, to be cherished, to be sustained. Clearly, the satisfactions of social success or unassailable security or even the trappings of control are not the acme of the good life. Those things vanish like the horizon on a misty day— once so surely there, now just as surely gone. It is the spiritual part, the elusive part, of the human enterprise that brings peace in the midst of turmoil, that does not strive to avoid the world but only to live in it well.

Sometime or other in every life comes the raw awareness that to live in a world ever clamoring, seldom settled, always in flux, it is only the depth of the spiritual well in us that can save us from the fear of our own frailty. And yet, ironically enough, the very challenges that wear us down, the very winds that threaten our stability of soul are also exactly what, by our confronting them, by our besting them, prepare us spiritually to face a muddled life with equanimity, with fortitude, with hope. But where can we start to become what we know, down deep, ourselves to be— spiritual seekers in search of a way through a serious period, an astounding eruption of normalcy in our lives?

In every age there are those who have known the road before us and passed its signs on. It is that kind of wisdom sunk in bedrock and tested by the centuries that we ourselves now need to discover. More than any of the things we've been assured for decades would be our lives' collateral—the certificates, the promotions, the money, the network of contacts—we need the things that last. We need depth of heart. We need stolidity of soul. We need what the forays of time cannot take away.

At this crossover point in every person's life emerges the need to prioritize our values. We need a way of living life and seeing life that brings more human entirety than it does popular acclaim. We need soul.

It is those things this book seeks to explore, to test, to offer for consideration as we grow from stage to stage, from emptiness to wholeness.

The truth is that every major spiritual tradition in the world has a monastic stream that feeds it. This book is for those who are not necessarily looking for a church or an ashram or a monastery or even a study group to join; they may already have one. They may not really want one. What they are looking for is simply the wholeness of their spiritual selves that dwells within them already, often overlooked until the well goes dry.

It is finding the rest of the self—the self we need most under pressure—that the monastic heart seeks out.

This small book carries the weight and wisdom of a great spiritual tradition into the twenty-first century. The Western tradition of monasticism has served all forms of the spiritual life—both individual and communal—across all cultures and all eras. It is a tradition that serves the seeker who desires a vibrant spiritual life but does not want to become the keeper of a system.

To invoke the insights of so revered a tradition invites the reader to understand the past, yes, but not to stay there. It beckons the serious spiritual seeker to examine an ancient lifestyle asking what it has that can enrich the present, once thought impermeable, now thought shattered.

Monasticism is the single-hearted search for what matters in life. Any life. Every life. It emerged in Rome in the shadow of a broken society centuries ago. It is possible, in the light of this period, that it has never been more needed than it is now.

Benedictine monasticism—Christian monasticism—was founded in the early days of the sixth century by a man of high ideals in search of personal growth and moral integrity. Benedict of Nursia came into Rome, the center of the empire, as a young student and found it eroded to the core, a broken and disappointing place. Disillusioned by the political corruption of Rome and the collapse of its character, he went off by himself to contemplate what to do next with his life.

In the end, Benedict never set out to conquer Rome. On the contrary. He set out to create a new way to live the good life in the shell of the old, in a society not unlike ours. Not unlike us. People from every rank, looking for security, stability, sanity, sanctity, flocked to this new way to live a totally human life, a life free from slavery, inequality, and dangerous individualism. And people have been flocking to it still, in our own time, in multiple ways, from various levels of society, all serious in their search for the good life, the happy life, the productive life, the holy life.

Clearly, when anything—any institution—lasts over fifteen hundred years, someone ought to ask what it has within it that can possibly go on from age to age. What is it that can respond to each era in turn and, at the same time, constantly attend to the distinct spiritual questions and quests of each?

The key to understanding this life in our own time is to realize that what is asked of us in this ancient Rule of Benedict is simply to begin to live an ordinary life extraordinarily well. We are not expected to leave society. We are meant to live in it in a new way, in a way that can survive the shifts and turns of the system because the soul is grounded in the ultimates of life rather than in its inessentials.

To withdraw from the chaos of an age is one way to create a new life, but isolation is not the only way to find a path to wholeness. Most of all, in this century of huge urban centers and digital connectedness, it is clearly no longer the most common way. Instead, we must each seek to discover what spiritual sanity means for us, so that whatever changes around us does not change our best longings, does not corrupt our best selves.

This book invites that reflection. To become what we seek to be for this age, we need to look at what each of the elements of the monastic mindset meant in its own age. Then, we will be prepared to maintain the tradition and, at the same time, expand it. We will be able to apply it to our own lives as so many have done before us over the centuries. We can offer this great, newly emerging moment of global transition in our own society the wisdom of the past on which to be grounded.

To live a mature spiritual life requires that we choose the values that will ground our hearts, stretch our vision, and give new energy to our hopes.

This little book will explore the elements of the monastic mindset. By coming to understand the basic components of the kind of life cultivated in monasteries for centuries, we may come to know the kind of spiritual and social consciousness needed now and here, as we grapple with the built-in uncertainties of a commercial world in the throes of philosophical division.

In our own time, then, we ourselves can grow in wisdom, equanimity, and strength of soul by refusing to be drawn into the clamor and chaos of a world on the brink. Then nothing of the raucous will be able to drown our souls in noise. Nothing of self-centeredness will blind us to the work of the Creator, who began creation but left it for us to complete. Nothing of the inherent beauty of life will be found in the grasping for life's gadgets.

While we look at the ways that have been used to cultivate a monastic heart for centuries, we can begin to reshape them for our own. Without going to a monastery, we can become, like those before us, deeper, freer selves—richer souls—and, as a result, bequeath to our world the most monastic twenty-first-century monastics of them all.

The pages that follow will present the components of monastic life and not only the impact it had on the human condition centuries ago but also the grounding of humanity and monasticism we are seeking yet today in our own lives, in our own ways.

So let us begin, as chapter 57 of the Rule of Benedict cites: "That in all things God may be glorified."

THE
MONASTIC
HEART

1

BELLS

On Remembering

**In every Benedictine monastery around the world,
bells and bell towers are a common part of the architecture—
even now when bells are no longer a common part
of human communication.**

Every afternoon, as I sit in my upstairs office, I hear the old
monastery bells begin to ring in the once Benedictine church
that then adjoined this inner-city monastery. In fact, the bells
from Benedictine monasteries everywhere still peal out around
the world. Our original monastery moved over 50 years ago from
an in-town property to the edge of the city. So we have another
bell tower and a new electronic carillon. The big old brass bell,
"Theodore," shipped here from Germany ages ago, now rests re-
tired and reverenced on a brick base in the memorial garden of the
new monastery. New bells go on ringing over our lakeside property daily, just as the old one did here in the inner city for more
than 150 years. No bedroom clocks, no personal watches take
their place as harbingers of spiritual time.

But why?

The monastic heart is a heart that goes through life on a wave
of common time. Its hours are counted out and set up in un-

changing and perpetual order. In the monastery, over and over again, every day of a monastic's life, the community bells mark the passing of the moment, of the work, of the hours of prayer, of our lifelong promises, of life's important things. No, we don't ring bells because monastics can't tell time. We ring them because we are as prone to being swept away from the center of life by all its tempest and trivia as is anyone else in the modern world.

The purpose of Benedictine bells is not to spell out the hour of the day at all; that task is left to horologists. Our bells, on the other hand, are there to wrench our attention back to what is really important in life: The memory of God in our midst. The memory of the purpose of life. The memory that time is moving on and so must we. The recognition that life today is different than life was yesterday and we must not try to hold life back. The bells jog the memory that there are actually more important, more meaningful, more demanding dimensions of life than anything ordinary we can possibly be doing as they ring.

The bells stop us in midflight to prod us to ask ourselves again if what we are doing is what we are really meant to be doing. But most of all, they are begging us to listen to the great issues of life, to the rest of life. They are asking us to hear the cries of those in need, to confront our own reservoirs of pain.

When loss drains the dregs of the heart, the bells remind us that another day is coming and with it the grace we need to confront it. When fear captures us, the bells are there to remind us not to be afraid. When the past has disappeared from our sights and there is not even a glimpse of the future to be found, the bells remind us that the only way to deal with the future is to accept its call to shape it.

Integrating the Practice

It's what you pay attention to in life that determines both your commitments and your inner happiness. Time is its indicator. One of the most important questions of life is surely, Where do I spend my time and what am I doing there? The second is, What calls me back to where I'm meant to be? Money? Work? The crowd? What . . . ?

Monastic bells can draw your attention again and again to what is really of great concern: the call of God in you to remember the suffering; to comfort the grieving; to feed the underfed; to continue the work of God's love for all the earth. If those are the bells of life that waken our hearts, then, perhaps, we will finally become a country again, a people again, families again, and reflect more signs of humanity than of nationalities and clans and colors.

Monastic bells are meant to remind you to get back up on your feet and go on.

It is time to reach across borders and backyard fences and family separations and refuse to allow politics and viruses and the hurts of the heart to destroy your humanity, your community, your role in life. The bells you choose to listen to deliberately interrupt what you're doing and make you listen to life as it goes on around you, to make you think again about what must be dealt with now if you are ever to go beyond the chaos that threatens you, beyond the pain and confusion within.

The questions should nag at you: What needs are around me? What pain, what sorrow, what grief must be dealt with before life can ever become life again? What is weighing me down? Here. In my private little world? Now.

The truth is that what consumes your thinking controls you. What is getting your attention now? Status? Personal success? Loss? Fear? Better yet, what *should* be getting your attention now?

The Benedictine bell is there to interrupt your distractions, to put you back on course.

When the sound of these bells rings in your heart a message of obligation, a signal of God's call to you to be aware of your task in life, then you shall have come to the point of spiritual adulthood. Then the presence of God will be a living, breathing grace in you. You will know that, whatever the struggle of doing what must be done, *you are being called to do it.* And doing it will change your little part of the world and make it better in the end.

Then the world will grow on because you have been here and listened to the bells call you to that other part of yourself where what you do really means something to someone. The bells remind you that though God created the world, God did not finish it. That part of creation was left to you and me to do for ourselves. For that great enterprise we all need a bell to ring us awake.

Bells and gongs bring the soul to attention. But they do more than that; they interrupt what is purposeless in life and focus your heart. They make you ask yourself what it is that is absorbing you now and, then, what it is that should be centering you now.

In every life there is something that takes more of your attention than anything else. Which brings you to the real question: Should it? What is really important now? What means more to you: the value of your work or the amount of money you get for doing it? Or, better yet, what is really more important to you: what you do to make a living or the way you live life when you're not working?

The truth is that we all need a bell: the one we set on our watches, the chime we put on the windowsill to invite the call of the wind. The one that's programmed on our cellphones to remind us to say a prayer for strength before we begin the first effort of the day. We need some kind of bell that not only distracts us from the worry, the irritation, the boredom, the fear, the disappointment of the day. We need something that calls us to something greater than the little worries of life and so brings our soul to its center again.

The important thing is that you put some sound into your life that stops you and turns you toward the real purpose of life. Then, when the tiny ring of it comes, you will pause long enough to thank God for life, to ask for the strength to commit yourself to a greater question than what the daily brings.

We each need a personal call at specific moments to point us to life as it should be, not simply life as it is. The bells remind us that though God created the world, God did not finish it.

2

STATIO

On Involvement

There is more to the spiritual life than keeping a schedule of
religious events. Merely attending such spiritual exercises is
not enough. We must take our whole selves there—mind and
heart—as well as our bodies. And we must be there five minutes before prayer starts.

I hadn't been long in the monastery until I noticed a basic logis-
tical fallacy. The bell for the various segments of prayer rang at
the proper hour. But, the novice director told us, we were to be in
chapel five minutes before the bell rang.

What?!

Statio is being where you are supposed to be before you need
to go there. In monastic parlance, it is about being consciously
committed to what you are there to do, so that your mind isn't
partially distracted by the thing you just left behind. It requires
you to get ready for one of these central moments of your spiritual
life, to concentrate on the things of God, to leave behind for a
while the distractions of the day. It enables us to separate ourselves
from one thing entirely before we start another one with half ourselves still concentrated on the thing we just left behind.

Monastic statio, going to chapel to get ready for prayer before prayer starts, is one of the important things in monastic life. Being prepared, conscious, alert, ready, centered, and there—early—is the lesson of a lifetime. We learn that to concentrate on words and phrases we've said for years is the beginning of spiritual maturity. It is a model of the manner of spiritual growth that develops a layer, an insight at a time.

It is the call to the person with a monastic heart to realize that we are about to do something life-changing, something that will take more than simple assent. It takes putting our hearts and our minds into the part of our lives—one monastic prayer period at a time—that will shape us over the years until we are one with it at all times. Not just at prayer times. It takes concentration on what we are about to do. It takes a commitment of time, of involvement, of special attention. Mine.

But the consequences of community statio don't stop with prayer periods. It's so easy to slough off the little things of life, like sending in the absentee voting form or signing on to a recommendation for more teacher's aides in the schools. We support it; we just don't do anything tangible to prove that. We're busy with other things. We stop thinking about it the minute it's over. We go to meetings, but we don't take the time to prepare for them. We don't follow up on the decisions that were made in them. We don't think the proposals through before the next meeting. We lack statio. Concentration. Preparation. Serious commitment to serious things.

Statio, giving my whole self to the present moment, is an exercise in consciousness. It means not running in and out of an event just to prove that I was there, that I went because it was on the calendar but not because I intend to give my best to climbing the summit at hand.

Statio—stopping to collect our hearts and minds before we begin something new—is the sign that we know we are about to do the will of God for the world. We know that we must not go at it when we are scattered of heart. We will not shirk our engagement. We must not go unprepared to do our best.

In spiritual language, the meaning is clear: We must give our whole selves to the spiritual meaning of the moment. Statio is not simply about making time for spiritual reflection. On the contrary. It's about really being where we are—conscious and committed—when we go. It's about living consciously. Whatever we do. Whoever we are.

So much in the pressured personal life of this era is done on the run. Is done while doing something else: like checking our email or making business calls from the car. Instead, statio is not only about being where we are. It's about getting there early and centering ourselves consciously.

It's about giving myself the time I need to grieve the loss of the beloved uncle or mentor or friend who died from the virus, not from old age. Death is a lesson in life that I need to absorb. Simply being active is not life. Statio tells me to take the time to think things over, to think things through, to stop rushing from one aimless remark to another. To know where I am; to think about what I'm doing. It tells us that we are here to create our lives, not to script them as if one page of patter fits all. Modern culture, on the other hand, rushes us from one activity to another, which, unfortunately, can become an excuse to let the hard moments of life go by unattended, unthought out.

Monastics give time to concentrating the soul on the very process of prayer so that prayer itself may shape us into real human, human beings. To notice the tears of another and stop to dry them, to hear the despair in a sister's voice and care enough to ask what's wrong is the statio of our lives. Little by little we begin to learn it by being serious about the statio that precedes prayers. It teaches us to focus on the important dimensions of life. Anything else is to turn ourselves into automatons without a soul.

Integrating the Practice

Statio is the monastic gift of taking a deep breath between things; going into the next personal encounter centered, quiet, and gathered of mind and heart. It calls you to calm down, to sink into the spiritual life with all your heart, all your mind, all the layers of the soul. It calls you to learn to be where you are, to stop checking the time *here* so that you can get *there* as quickly as possible and so miss everything that's going on *here*—right now.

Gathering yourself between the major moments of life calls you to decant yourself. It teaches you to enjoy the emptiness of time rather than simply fill it with a ritual. It asks you to be present to your own needs and trust the God who will now guide you from within. It asks you to become a fully human, human being in a world that has learned to recite the texts of the moment rather than to bring honest sensitivity to every prayer segment of the day. Learning to calm your heart before striking out in emotional darkness is one of the most important dimensions of every response in life.

It's the lack of statio—of sober consideration of what's happening—that starts road rage. It's the lack of the spirit of statio that turns misunderstandings into lifelong enmities. It's the lack of internal quiet and focus that sends you into confusion of thought and chaos of soul.

Yoga is meant to concentrate you. Meditation is meant to center you. And statio is meant to take you down into a depth of spirit so that you bring every bit of yourself to the moment at hand. It takes you into the well of life, where you can find the best

of yourself in the midst of the melee of modern noise—the blare
of horns, the burst of sirens.

For the average person, statio is not about being in chapel five
minutes before Vespers. Instead, more than likely it's about attending to the world around you. It's about more than saying
you're concerned about what is happening to vulnerable members
of the population. It's about taking time to study the issues. It's
about getting ready to continue the conversation, so that those
who have no voice have yours.

**Statio, giving your whole self to the present moment, is an
exercise in consciousness. Statio, stopping to collect your heart
and mind before you begin something, is the sign that you
know you are about to do the will of God for the world.**

3

ANTIPHON

On Mantras of the Moment

**An antiphon is a refrain that begins and ends each of the
psalms, which form the major content of the monastic office.
It is meant to distill the psalm into a single idea that
can be pondered and understood.**

I remember even the weight of the prayer book that the sisters
handed us on our first day in the monastery and that we used at
every time of community prayer. We were the new postulants and
we didn't have a clue what we were doing, let alone how to pray.
An "angel," the older novice assigned to help each of us find our
way through the segments of community prayer, pointing at the
Latin text, reaching over us to turn the proper pages, completely
negated the purpose of the help. I was distraught. I didn't know
then that learning the 150 psalms we said every week would take
a lifetime. I also didn't know that there would be an easier way to
do it. Paying attention to the antiphons would become the lifeline
of my soul.

Antiphons bracket off one kind of moment from another.
They enable us, then, to deal with one great message after another.
They distill the essence of the message. "O God, be my defense,"
one antiphon of one psalm says. Another declares, "I was up to

my neck in seaweed and you, O God, saved me." A third reminds the community, "Sing a song of praise to God who has saved us and set our feet upon the rocks." Which means that we leave prayer aware of three central ideas rather than of sixty separate lines of them: first idea, that God protects us; second idea, that even the worst parts of life will not defeat us; third idea, that in the end, life will calm again.

Antiphons, in fact, guide us both through the psalms and *into* the psalms at the same time. In essence, antiphons allow us to separate one major idea from another, to concentrate on one at a time, rather than get confused by trying to deal with every line of all of them at once. As a result, antiphons become models of how to deal with our own lives.

Monastics gather several times a day to pray the psalms together. Various segments or "hours," called the Divine Office, are parceled out a day, an hour, at a time until the entire psalter of 150 psalms completes the week. But it's not the number of psalms we say that counts. The real issue lies in the fact that the psalms deal with every social-emotional dimension of human growth and struggle: celebration, mourning, fear, loss, praise, hope, faith, confusion, disappointment, struggle—whatever. To get in touch with those human responses is to become more fully human ourselves. The psalms can do that for us.

The psalms are really ancient poems. They speak of joy and suffering, hope and despair, beauty and sorrow, faith and trust in hard times. They speak of everything we've ever felt in life. To pray the psalms, then, is to confront life in all its fury, all its faith. Which is exactly where the importance of having the antiphon comes in. Monastics know that though life is a procession of joys and sorrows, we cannot allow ourselves to be overwhelmed by them all at one time. We have to come to realize that life is an exercise in multiple kinds of joy and sorrow—each with its own meaning and power.

Antiphons school us to concentrate on the major idea of a psalm. Antiphons also school us in the ability to face one part of life at a time. Each moment, each idea gives us new depth, new understanding, and a new sense of faith. We are not expected to absorb every dimension of the psalm in its entirety; rather, the antiphon tells us the major idea of the psalm so we can deal with its essential message rather than remember every detail of the explanation. When we live by experiencing and understanding one emotion, one idea at a time, we soon know in the deepest part of our souls that we can live through the next great spiritual messages of life to come as well.

Integrating the Practice

Similar to you, the writers of the psalms knew what it felt like, what it is to be overwhelmed by life, by the shock of death, or by the total powerlessness that a pandemic or war or tragedy brings. The psalmists knew what it is to be on the edge of emotional fatigue or economic collapse or the social paralysis that comes with fear of the inevitable and relentless future.

And yet, in the psalms one hard moment of life after another is bracketed. Every great trial of life is set off from the rest of life's circumstances so that one difficult thing does not obscure all the other good things of life. Will you absorb the idea of Psalm 3, that death is difficult to accept? Yes—and you can also concentrate on the truth of Psalm 4, that God will carry you through it. In your own time, by bracketing life's moments, you know that you must struggle with a pandemic, yes—and, the psalmists assure you, you do not have to succumb to this danger or in fact any other.

Antiphons teach you that you must learn to keep sight of all the facets of your life so that you can stay both realistic and healthy at the same time. You will endure today praying, "God be with me as I face this moment," as the antiphon says. And yet, the antiphon reminds you that God has been with you in all your trials and, at the same time, settled you in a garden of goodness to strengthen you for just this moment.

You will not compress the full meaning of life in any one moment. You will face them all, one antiphon at a time. By learning to deal with the great spiritual ideas of life, you become strong enough—when confronted with great moments of your own—to trust the loving presence of God in your life, as the psalmists did in theirs.

The antiphon functions like a mantra. It pockets the moment in one small piece of memory and then, like grace, moves into another very different moment. In the end, you realize that life is made up of many ideas, many emotions, many ways of seeing, not just one. It is an exercise in mental health to refuse to surrender to any one of them in one fell swoop. It is healthy to meet life one great moment at a time and learn how to grow from insight to insight. Yes, there is a great deal of pain and loss, of evil and obstruction to be experienced in life, but no one segment of it needs to destroy you if you only remember all the other moments as well.

Antiphons give life to you by doling out one realization after another so that you do not surrender and shrivel from the glut of them. The practice of antiphons is clear: You are not called to memorize the psalms in order to know them. Instead, you are taught to imbibe them, one drop at a time.

In praying the psalms and writing antiphons for the great moments of life, you protect yourself from becoming overwhelmed by the surfeit of them on your heart: "God be with me as I face

the death of my loved one," the antiphons teach you to pray . . .
"God protect me as I take this test," you remember . . . "God give
me the strength to trust You in the dark places of life," you
plead . . . "God give me hope enough to begin again."

It is in marking off your life in antiphons—in segments—that
you will see God most clearly one day at a time and life as a cataract of gifts and graces, of crises and challenges that, eventually,
bring you to the fullness of growth.

**You will not compress the full meaning of life in any one mo-
ment. You will face them all, one antiphon at a time. By learning to deal with the great spiritual ideas of life, you become
strong enough—when confronted with great moments of your
own—to trust the loving presence of God in your life, as the
psalmists did in theirs.**

4

MONASTIC PROCESSION

On the Display of Oneness/Unity

On great feast days of the Church calendar and special
community events, the sisters come into chapel in procession.
We walk two by two out of the community room, through
the cloister walk to the chapel, down the center aisle to the
altar. There the sisters bow first to the Book of the Gospels
and then, turning to face their partners, they bow a long,
slow bow before going to their individual pews.

It is a slow and solemn procession for, it would seem, no reason
at all but ritual.

I remember watching church processions all my young life as
great feast days of every year followed one another in regal display.

The yearly parish Commemoration of the Forty Hours' Devotion was an ever-increasing presentation of clerical pomp and circumstance. The long line of priests came down the aisle in
seniority: With the bright brass processional cross leading the
way, boy choristers in bright red gowns were followed by page
boys in pantaloons, then altar boys, seminarians, priests in order
of ordination, and finally monsignors in maroon cassocks preced-
ing the candle bearers, the incense bearer carrying the smoking

censer filled with incense, and, finally, under the canopy, the celebrant, usually a bishop with cape trailing in the hands of young pages, and the monstrance, the gold cross that displayed the Blessed Sacrament, held high over his head.

It was beautiful, stirring, effective. You knew that you were in the presence of power. That these were important people. That this was an otherworldly moment. It was the male church walking by, full of authority, full of mystery and mystique.

The procession of women Benedictines, in contrast, is a completely other event. It says that these are simple people who recognize the simple, holy beauty of the other.

It's a very solemn event, too, this gentle kind of community procession. Especially when the community in procession, like mine, is a basically easygoing, friendly group. Our procession is not about our ranking; instead, it celebrates the sense of community that has held this group of vowed women together for years, centuries even, if you consider all the decades of sisters who have walked down their community aisles together before this. One thing is for certain, this procession of women Benedictines is not about the celebration of power.

In this case, the community is not rigidly or extremely formal about anything. It is not a display of important people. It is a display of a very important kind of relationship. It is a presentation of the kind of community that comes out of the same mindset, the same notion of holiness, the same bonds to one another, the same commitment to the world and its people around them.

This community goes through life as comfortably with street people as with wealthy benefactors, and there are many of each. These sisters are well educated and very effective women. But simplicity, not the trappings of power, marks their very powerful presentation of human community. Here everybody is welcome. Here everybody comes and feels at home.

Nevertheless, on feast days, the community does not come in one at a time and take their usual seats. The community as community forms into a tight group when the bell rings and, with random partners, marches into chapel to the sound of the organ and slowly and solemnly bows very, very deliberately, to one another. To one another. Think about it. These are women without rank, with little or no public or political power. And they are saying what by this procession?

First, they are saying that their shared equality makes them a powerful group. It is what they do together that makes their voices heard, their commitments clear. People join a group to do together what they know cannot possibly be done alone—like grow in holiness or give themselves away for the needs of others.

Second, such a procession says that everybody here has melded into a new kind of family. When they first arrived, they were actually strangers to one another. Yet, each of them a stranger, they were taken in as if they had been together for years. We lived together, we worked together, we ran the community laundry together, and in all the other little things of life, we got to know one another as—yes—"sisters."

Third, the procession is a lesson about what is really sacred in life. It is the persons on whose support we each depend, of course, but more than that, it is the individuals, the persons, who themselves alone are sacred beings. Meant to be revered. Accepted for who and what they are. It is, actually, a stunning expression of what it means to be a community: strong, effective, alive, an unbreakable bearer of the beauty of acceptance and common heart.

As young sisters we had been taught also to bow our heads to one another as we passed each other in the silent hallways. But bowing heads to one another was not a comfortable American custom. In more recent generations of American novices, the nod of the head passed quietly away. But even if unconsciously, the meaning of the moment, respect and personal bonding, had grown deep monastic roots, where smiles and the meeting of the eyes became the gentle acknowledgments of the other.

Monasticism is about the creation of the common heart and communal support. It does not depend on status or power or exceptionalism for its effectiveness. On the contrary, it depends for its efficacy only on its common search, its single commitment, its joint efforts, and its spiritual energy. It says that none of us are alone. When the moment of need comes, someone—a stranger, perhaps—will be there to hold us up.

Integrating the Practice

Through this practice of deliberately recognizing and revering the humanity in one another, you will see how important it is to be sister to the one who is not your sister, to give yourself away to those to whom you owe nothing at all but loving concern for people who need you. And so, in procession, you bow to the other. When you do, you recognize the self-giving of the other. You remember the words of the One who said, "What you do unto others, you do unto me." And you revere the goodness of the sisters who are models of that to the rest of us.

I often wonder what it would do to the marriage ceremony for the bride and groom to bow to the sacredness of the other one. I wonder what it would say to the children of a family to see their parents bow to one another every morning, every evening. I wonder what it would do to the self-esteem of a child to have the parents clasp the palms of their hands together as they bow to the child in a gesture that speaks of the sacredness of the child herself.

I wonder what it says to the lonely in the chapel, to the fearful in the congregation, to those who come to the monastery to see the recognition of goodness given to one another in a world where "rugged individualism" is considered a value instead of a loss. Imagine the awareness, the glow of the sacred, the sight of the holy, the kind of reverence that people might take to every relationship, every stranger, thereafter. Maybe all these years of bowing to one another say more than we consciously recognize: That the other is sacred. That the other is to be revered. That the other is welcomed.

To create a world that sees the humanity of one another, we must see that humanity first. Surely the way we regard the other is the way the world we create around us will also come to regard, respect, and ennoble others, too. Then we are all upheld—consciously, clearly, publicly. And all of that in one simple procession. One simple bow to another, who before the bow came was secretly hurting, secretly lonely, secretly in need, but now, finally, feels worthy. Not powerful or important. Yet something more meaningful than that. To the person with the burdens of failure or abandonment or rejection to carry, a bow to them may be the reminder they have been waiting for of their eternal, universal worth.

That one bow, that simple bow you give to another, is a monastic gift of ultimate meaning. It says quite clearly: Together we are one; do not be afraid. Even better is the awareness that a bow is something you can do wherever you are: with the family, on the street corner, to the ones who have lived in a wheelchair all their life. A bow of the head. A quiet nod. A wave of the hand. A smile to someone you do not know. A gesture of awareness. And care.

Try it—and feel the beat of your monastic heart.

Monasticism is about the creation of the common heart and communal support. It does not depend on status or power or exceptionalism for its effectiveness. When the moment of need comes, someone—a stranger, perhaps—will be there to hold us up.

5

THE RULE OF BENEDICT

On Seeking God

Written in the sixth century, the Rule of Benedict is the oldest document in the Western world on the structure and purpose of religious life and its search for God. It presents both a defined spirituality and a way of life to make it real rather than simply a poetic presentation of a fanciful vision.

There are few institutions that did as much for any geographic region as Benedictine monasteries did for Europe across the centuries. They brought a Rule and a way of life that was balanced, ordered, realistic, and, most of all, humane. This was a Rule, a monastic lifestyle, that could be trusted to build communities that fed the people, educated them, healed them, even protected them in their round towers in case of siege.

Monasticism restored the society around it, by first developing a corps of spiritual seekers, monastics, who were strong of heart themselves, in touch with the spirit of God within them, and open to dealing with the needs of those around them. They were strong of soul enough then to carry the world around them as well as their own lives and future.

Whatever the move toward sin and neuroticism that came

with negativity and guilt as the Church declared the bubonic plague a punishment for sin, the sixth-century Rule of Benedict never wavered in its certainty that the will of God for people was that they be the best human beings that a human being could be. That people, like you and me, would not only value human development but extend that concern to the world around them.

As the Church became more institutionalized and so more divided, monasticism went on maintaining that life was meant to be a relationship between the individual and God, not between the individual and any particular system. Whatever the call to win the war between then-emerging denominations, monasticism simply ignored it as a barrier to holiness and steered a straight line from an individual's soul to the heart of God.

Benedict's model of a holy life, a peaceful life, and a productive life became the single model of organized religious life until the twelfth century.

Benedict of Nursia, a young man who was himself disillusioned and disturbed by the corrupt society of his day, developed cenobitic monasticism—communal monasticism—as an antidote to inequality, narcissism, injustice, classism, and oppression. In his communities the monastics lived in stable groups, supported themselves, and carried on an ordered life of prayer, work, and community under the guidance of the Rule and an Abbot or Abbess/Prioress.

Four major characteristics marked this new order then and mark it still. Hospitality, productivity, community, and immersion in God gave Benedictines what no other religious groups of the time could provide. They were stable. They were agents of social change. They lived a communal—a family—life. They had one major commitment: "To Seek God." Not only was God the center of their personal lives but God was also the center of the community life itself. Benedictine lives were a model for all the world to see—and come to expect. By the ninth century, Charlemagne and Benedict of Aniane had pronounced the Benedictine Rule the norm of religious life. Why? Because it was socially productive and self-sustaining, internally well organized and spiritually rich. Benedictine monasteries were at the center of every village and fast becoming assets to the larger society. Monastic communities became the hospices, the hospitals, the educators, the scriptoriums, the public mediators, and the judicial systems of the village square.

They were productive.

It was monastics who engaged and trained the serfs and peasants who clustered around the growing monasteries looking for work. The monks tilled the land, built the buildings and churches, developed agriculture and husbandry, and, eventually, became the major economic engines of their regions.

These were not religious who came and went. These were religious who came and stayed; who came and changed whole tracts, whole valleys, whole areas for the better. These monasteries were stable. Whatever happened to the areas around them happened to them. If disease and plague attacked the region, it was incumbent on the monastery to take an active part in its purge. If education was lacking, it was important that the monks open schools to train the next generation in what the present one already knew. If the streams went dry, the monastery participated in the development of irrigation techniques. If law and order collapsed, it was the monastics who became the unbiased judges who could be trusted to put the area back together again. Finally, of course, the monasteries became the spiritual centers of the local communities as well.

Integrating the Practice

In your time, monasticism has spread around the world, still following the sixth-century Rule of Benedict, which began it. Your
task is to discover what monasticism has that has enabled it to last
for over fifteen centuries, still green, still fresh, still alive and growing. Most important of all, this tradition calls on you to do the
same now, when old social structures are collapsing around you
and new ones are badly needed. When your own personal spiritual life is seeking new direction and your soul is thirsting for
higher and deeper purpose and pursuits, monasticism offers an
age-old path still new, still vibrant.

Unlike the swings toward spiritual extremism and perfection-
ism that shook the Church as the centuries went by, the Rule of
Benedict offers normalcy as the will of God. This is a guide, a way
to heaven, that asks only what is doable.

Monastics seek one God, not necessarily one church or one
denomination. Monastics know that people go to God by different paths. The important thing to Benedictine monastics is to
remember that, in your own search, "ordinariness"—not spiritual
specialness—becomes the route to God.

The Rule of Benedict offered a way of life that brought spirit
and order to a world in crisis, and it can do the same for you
today. It concentrated on both internal personal growth and public development in a broken world. And to this day it goes on
strengthening the spine of the world, one person at a time. The
Rule calls you to fullness of life and concentrates you on the ideals
and interactions that make it possible, not only for yourself but
for the world around you.

Monasticism gave the world what the world needs now. It
shaped the lives of many, raised the spiritual standards for all, built
community, and developed the foundation for human growth

and national unity. It can do the same for you, both individually and communally. It is only a matter of cultivating within ourselves the elements of life and the insights of the spiritual mind that enable it.

The Rule of Benedict immerses you in the presence of God so that you may never forget that God's work must be your work and your work must be good for everyone you touch.

Benedictines have one major commitment in life: "To Seek God." Not only was God the center of their personal lives but God was also the center of the community life itself.

6

HORARIUM

On Parsing Time

The horarium of a monastery is the schedule of the day. It marks the way we divide our lives. There will be some time for prayer, some time for contemplation, some time for work, some time spent in common, some free time.

The modern age is a time of frenzy, pressure, deadlines, and overlapping elements of life: Home gets short shrift because of the late hours at work, the spiritual life becomes more recitation than reflection, family becomes Sunday lunch if we're lucky, life becomes one long exercise in catch-up activities.

If anything seems strange in the modern world now, it is the very thought of being able to manage time in a frenetic society. But to be young in the monastery before Vatican II was to live the community horarium as if simply being on time for everything was the essence of life. "A time for everything; everything in its own time" said it all. And in those days, each of those special segments of life could be lived daily. For almost everyone. We got up at the same time, ate breakfast together—at the same time—got into the van to be taken to the schools at which we taught—together. This life was an ordered one: Monastic days were divided into periods of prayer, work, study, and rest.

It wasn't static, but it was uniform and its teachings were clear. There was a way to live life: one way, no other. To live life well, it should be defined and scheduled, thank you. After all, farmers did, mothers did, assembly line workers did, everybody did. But things have changed now. Living in lockstep is a thing of the past, even, in large part, in monasteries, where monastics work different hours in different places. What is not different is that every one of those elements—prayer, contemplation, work, common time, and free time—has priority. And yet, how do any of us live life sensibly and sanely in a world where night never comes and the day is never over and everybody can do almost everything at any time they like? There is something about the division of the monastic day that has become a singular departure from contemporary life in the Western world. It is, at the same time, a singular gift.

Fifteen hundred years ago, when Benedict wrote his Rule for monastics, many of them could not read, and even if they could read, candles to read by were both expensive and difficult to come by. Most of all, they were a thousand years away from the invention of portable watches. Point: Sunlight ruled the day. "Make haste while the sun shines" was not a metaphor for productivity; it was a life lesson about doing the right things at the right time.

The monastic horarium kept life in balance. It guaranteed that every important dimension of life would be lived every day of the year. The community rose in the dark to pray the psalms they had memorized during the day. They went to bed on the brink of night and did community tasks "while the sun shone." On feast days, of which there were many in the liturgical calendar, and Sundays, they rested. It was the horarium that put all of life in place: rest, prayer, study, agricultural work, and building projects that sustained the community and served its neighbors.

Since that time, since the invention of the lightbulb, nothing has been quite the same. For any of us. We have extended daylight to the point where life is a twenty-four-hour-a-day proposition. We sleep when we can; we eat when there's nothing else to do; we work when we can get it in; we live on a merry-go-round of possibilities. The problem is that those errant, unscheduled schedules are shattering our souls.

Everything is without boundaries. Most of all, us. And there's the problem. When everything can be everywhere and anytime, it's too easy to discover it nowhere at all. And so we slip through life like bouncing balls. Here today, there tomorrow, nowhere specific much of the time.

To have a fixed time for beginning and ending the day is some help, a kind of anchor in the midst of a rolling sea. But the rest of life is still anybody's guess. And the rest of life is exactly where the stress is, in the emotional exhaustion that comes with confusion, in the loss of direction, in the lack of satisfaction, in the sheer uncertainty of it all.

It's when freedom isn't freedom at all that the confusion of time soon becomes a confusion of soul. It doesn't take long to figure out that to have no fixed time for the major parts of life is to have bartered our freedom away. No freedom to grow up in a family that schedules the daily family meal with all the warmth of presence and all the smells of fresh bread that implies. No freedom to visit a beloved grandmother who talks wisdom instead of money. No freedom to sit down and read a good book. In fact, nobody's free now to take the time to make the dinner, to mix the bread, to sit down together during the evening to review the day, to visit, to read light materials, to invite friends over for Sunday lunch.

The liturgy of family life at the family table has disappeared. So then where do we go for wisdom, for experience, for the fun it takes to laugh and the kind of support it takes to be allowed to cry on the shoulders of others rather than cry dry tears alone?

Integrating the Practice

In a world of lightbulbs, isn't a horarium a straitjacket that simply ties one down and makes the great plethora of possibilities impossible? And yet, look at us without a horarium: Can we really keep up at the rate we're going?

It's the horarium, the scheduling of the major parts of life, that enables you to become fully human over time, to take the time to live wholly, not spasmodically. It's a routine that gives you somewhere to go when life is lacking boundaries and a sense of what it means to have a purpose. Knowing that you'll be able to be with someone somewhere when you really need them is the only guarantee you have of love, life, and access to happiness. And yet, if you have no agreement on activities or docket of contacts to depend on, what are you but a rolling stone on your way down a pathless life? Monastic life, in the Benedictine tradition, says that the life of either family or individual development that leaves prayer, contemplation, work, community, or holy leisure out of the daily agenda is going dry from the inside out.

The ordered life is a life that has time for growth, for leisure, for study, for community, for reflection built into it, not grabbed on the fly. It plots a purpose and pursues it. It determines the self it wants and needs to be. It establishes life on a principle of wholesome self-development.

I see it every day in community: the sister who is still studying Spanish in her eighties; the sisters who are beginning to practice how to give conferences on the Internet, how to bring people together, how to reach out to other groups doing the same things. I hear about teachers who are learning to teach visually in a period of coronavirus so that their students are not left behind. At the same time, the world is full now of adults who are trying to save the economy from their dining room tables.

It is the horarium that plants in you all the diverse and divine parts of life and then helps you plot to keep the time and means it will take to find yourself in all of them.

It is knowing how to make and follow a horarium that will keep your private and professional worlds on a steady and an even keel.

The horarium keeps reflection—your relationship with God, your obligations to the world and community, your obligations to your own development and the care of those around you—constant and consistent. It is the key to staying open of heart and mind, to flourishing in hard times when answers are in flux, and to keeping yourself socially connected, psychologically healthy, and spiritually alive. To stumble through life without knowing where you're going next, let alone why, is the first step to inner disorientation. Running through your tiny little world in circles is no way to help balance either your own life or the health of the human enterprise.

Monastic life signals to you that order is not rigidity. It is the freedom you need to become the whole of yourself. It is the internal monitor that keeps you alive and growing—no matter how many viruses, how much stress, how much time there is to fill.

On the contrary, it is time itself—the horaria you make for yourself—that gives you the freedom to be pointed to your fulfillment and the roads that will take you there.

It's the horarium, the scheduling of the major parts of life, that enables us to become fully human over time, to take the time to live wholly, not spasmodically.

7

HOSPITALITY

On a Spirit of Welcome

Openness to the world—hospitality—is the monastic answer
to the needs of the world around it. The monastic's attempt
to create a new way of living in the shell of the old does
not excuse the monastic from the obligations of life. On the
contrary.

It's an interesting phenomenon: Monastic communities create
horaria designed to support a monastic way of life—balanced,
reflective, orderly, constant—and laypeople whose lives are mostly
lived in tatters stream to the monasteries to taste such order. In
fact, you can't be in a monastery very long before you realize that
there is always someone there besides the members of the community. (Pandemics excepted.) People come to pray with the
community, to spend some time in the hermitages, to make a re-
treat with a sister-director, to celebrate the great feasts, to withdraw from their own daily lives for a while. Guests are a large part
of any monastery. The Rule of Benedict in the sixth century devoted a whole segment to it. Why? Because monastic hospitality
is the bridge between two worlds—the monastic and the secular—
for the sake of both.

To talk about community and then hide from it would be an aberration of the monastic spirit. To live in a monastic community is to set out to inject life with a different mindset, a different way of being alive. It is not an exercise in flight from reality. It is an enterprise of the open heart.

Monastic hospitality is more than tea and cookies in the monastery parlor. It is not a social exercise. It is meant to allow people the experience of life without social chaos, interruption, and the internal noise that comes with all of that. It is an attempt to meet life on monastic terms: to give respite, to probe the spirit, to cleanse the clamor from the soul.

The Rule of Benedict has an engaging way of presenting its spirituality of hospitality. This sixth-century document reads, "Let an old monastic be placed at the door of the monastery, one who cannot run around, so that when any person comes, the porter—the gatekeeper—will say *'Benedicite,'* God bless you." Or in modern parlance, "Bless you for coming to interrupt our perfect lives." Or, "Thank you for saving us from being out of touch with the very people we need to be aware of and hear from and learn from and uphold."

That Benedicite rings in my ears every time I hear it. I shrink at the sight of headlines about closing our nation's borders to certain kinds of people from certain kinds of places. The fact is, I remember that my family, too, were those "certain kinds of people" who came from "certain kinds of places." They were Irish peasants from the bogs. They were Catholics seeking life in a Protestant country. They were young men running away from the famine and a sickened land. They were young women leaving a homeland where only men could inherit and women were left to fend for themselves. So they did. All of them left for the Irish ghettos of New York City and Boston, the railroad towns of

Pennsylvania, and the gold rush—the get-rich-quick cure for poverty—in California, which was gone before they got there. They all needed hospitality, help, welcome. Which, incidentally, are very monastic things.

In the sixth century, the Roman legions—the military that had extended the empire's borders and defended its walls—were disappearing. It was costing more to maintain the legions than they could extract from colonies already bled dry by taxation. Rome itself was defenseless as a result, and pilgrims were prey to every robber and rapist on the unguarded roads. But monasteries, in the name of hospitality, rose up to fill that gap by building a chain of hospices. The Benedictine boast was that it was possible for travelers to cross Europe and stay in a Benedictine guesthouse every night along the way, welcome and secure. Inclusion of the needy, the defenseless, the poor, the sick was part of the monastic contribution to the development of the very concept of human community in an extremely tribal world.

Hospitality was not a social nicety for monastics. It was a ministry, an act of mercy, a response to the reckless generosity of Jesus. Centuries later, monasteries still open their doors to students, to families, to travelers everywhere. Hospices, hermitages, monastery visits from strangers and travelers are still common everywhere. Indeed, the Rule was clear then—and is still clear now. It guides all of us. It says: "Guests are to be received as Christ." They were to be met by every member of the community. They were to be seated at the head table for meals. They were to receive a blessing when they came in the door and a blessing when they left.

Hospitality is meant to be civilization making. It is the model of inclusion. It is the foundation for world peace in its openness everywhere to everyone, no racial, national, religious credentials necessary. Hospitality interrogates each and all of us yet about our own acceptance of the foreigner, the stranger, the seeker, the lost, the ones who are not like us, who may well be "certain kinds of people from certain kinds of places." Hospitality calls us to standards of humanity which communicate clearly that welcome is our brand. Regardless.

Integrating the Practice

Hospitality calls us to communicate dignity and respectability to those whom others may consider unacceptable not because they lack soul but because they have no ways to dress it up. We welcome those whom others refuse to care for simply because "they're not our kind of people." They are all people, you see; just not "our kind."

To take someone into the home, the country, the job, your life, and fail to make them comfortable, to care for them well, is to fail at the very basic level of humanity. Strangers are to be made secure, not made beholden to you, not made to grovel with gratitude. By being with you, they are meant to know, to feel what it really means to be accepted. As Carl W. Buehner has said, "They may forget what you said—but they will never forget how you made them feel."

That is exactly what hospitality does for the person who is lucky enough to receive it. And it's what hospitality does for the giver, for you and me, who already know ourselves to be safe, to be worthy, to be cared for; that is life-changing.

Bedouins, nomadic herders in the desert, always sat with their tent flaps open, we're told—just in case a stranger in need of water would come their way. Just in case they might someday need water themselves. Hospitality secures peace in a system. It makes us all potential friends. It saves you and me from the soul-corroding threats of suspicion and skepticism that those who come across our borders hear from us a hundred miles before they even get here.

Then, if we are lucky, if we are brave, if we are open to Jesus in disguise, having trusted the first stranger, we gather the courage to open our lives to the next. We lose the irrational fears that plague us about people who are different from you and me. We begin to see in others the very responses we see in ourselves: joy, pain, fear, desperation, need, hope, ability, commitment, love, and relentless attempts to succeed at the fine art of being human. We see the crying children, the exhausted mothers, the heavy-laden men who carry the few items they and their families were able to bring with them. If any.

We begin, then, to try to get to know the other before we judge them, before we label them, before we allow the very fact that they come from different roots than we do to ignore them, expel them, deny them the opportunities we had to get ahead in life. Then we take their children out of cages, their exhausted women out of the long lines of beggars, their men out of our detention centers, where they have been put without cause.

Then we become more human ourselves. We free ourselves from the tension, the fear, the stress that comes from defending ourselves against enemies that are not there.

And, most of all, we cry aloud that others may see the persons behind the dusty feet and tangled hair, the tired eyes and stained jackets, and say to them, as does the old monk in the Rule, "Benedicite."

Thank you for prying open our hearts so that our souls may be saved.

Hospitality is meant to be civilization making. It is the model of inclusion. It is the foundation for world peace in its openness everywhere to everyone, no racial, national, religious credentials necessary. Hospitality interrogates each and all of us still about our own acceptance of the foreigner, the stranger, the seeker, the lost, the ones who are not like us.

8

CHOIR

On Singing Praise

Choir is a term that describes the prayer style of a monastic community. All the hours of the liturgical offices of the day are said aloud in community in dialogue style. One side recites a verse of the psalm and the other side answers it with the next verse. Prayer in choir symbolizes the whole Church crying out in praise and prayer, in confession and petition, in gratitude and need to God.

Prayer is not just praying in a monastery. It is not simply recitation of anything. In a monastery prayer is a way of life that integrates the great values of the faith with the life we breathe. It is not something tacked on to the day. It is the heartbeat of life, and it comes in many forms.

In the monastic community, for instance, there are two major types of prayer—community prayer and private prayer. Different in format, each has a special value, a special place in the spiritual development of the community and the individual monastic.

Community prayer is choral and dialogical. It is prayed by the entire community, one choir answering the other in one voice, a minimum of three major hours a day. Some monasteries pray both the major and minor offices together, as the ancient Rule requires.

The number of times a monastic community prays together is not the true value of the exercise. The purpose of communal prayer is to read the psalms and the scriptures together over and over every day in every monastery until they sink into our souls like the air we breathe.

It is the daily drip, drip, drip of the scriptures into the hearts and minds of every member of the community—years after those scriptures were gathered and formed into books—that forms the soul and the heart of the monastic. The Hebrew scriptures, the Gospels, the Letters of the Christian scriptures, and the psalmists' cries of praise and lament echo the human condition across the ages.

The concerns of Benedictine monastics of the past for justice, for joy, for community, for peace, for support, for answers to the needs of the day are our concerns still. The psalms that spoke to the urgencies of the world then speak to ours now as well. They ring through our lives forever, so that the monastic heart keeps both a clear focus on the hungers of humanity and a deep commitment to personal spiritual maturity. Sanctity, we know, is not a gesture of the moment. It is the continuing awareness of what it means to be committed to the will of God now and for all time.

The second kind of monastic prayer is private prayer: the response of the individual, of you and me, to the demands of the human condition and the will of God for the present. Interestingly enough, the Rule of Benedict warns the monastic community to "keep choral prayer short" so that its members have the time it takes to absorb the wisdom and reflect on each and every liturgy in ways that are familiar and meaningful.

But there are greater, more universal learnings that come from simply watching a community assemble for community prayer day after day after day for years. They come to say the same words, hear the same lessons, and wrestle with the same tensions now as those ideas conjured up over the years to community after community along the way.

Just as we eat the same foods all our lives, we say the same prayers to nourish our souls, to make sure we don't forget what's convenient for us to ignore. It is the rolling thunder of consciousness that forms us and will not allow us to pretend that we have forgotten what we do not want to remember.

Monastic prayer confronts us daily with ideas we do not understand and so must wrestle to the ground of our souls. It calls us to face the pain and anger in our own hearts, the kind of anger psalmists across the ages dealt with, too. In that way monastic prayer grows over the years, one versicle, one reading, one Gospel at a time. Then, little by little, we become the prayers we say.

Spirituality is not a sporadic exercise. It comes in getting up every morning with the Word of God stretching our hearts to see new things as well as to see old things that are needed newly in this time and place.

Most of all, perhaps, the monastic realizes by joining the group prayer over and over again that none of us are alone in the quest for the fullness of the spiritual life. Instead, we always have someone to talk to about the difficulty, the demands, because those someones have been sitting beside us all our lives. They are our spiritual directors on the Way.

Just as private prayer focuses us largely on ourselves, communal prayer opens us up to the will of God for the world—of which we are meant to be factors. Then, in the end, we become the prayer we are immersed in—just in the face of injustice, merciful in the face of need, compassionate in the face of pain, and peaceful in the face of struggle.

Prayer is a journey into the heart from which we emerge full of the love of God, the justice of God, and God's same goodwill for everyone.

Integrating the Practice

I asked young preprofessed sisters once why they went to prayer with the community every day, and I got the most impressive yet saccharine answers I could ever have imagined: "Because I love God"; "Because prayer is essential for everyone"; "Because it is deepening my relationship with Jesus." "No, no, no," I said to them answer after answer. Finally, one of them, exasperated, had the good sense to stop the merry-go-round. "If none of those answers are right," she said, "then why do we go to community prayer?" "We go to prayer," I said, "because the bell rings."

I could see their shock at the simplicity, the obvious clarity of the answer. Monastics go to community prayer because it is time for community prayers and those wonderful life-stopping bells call us there. The fact is that the community carries us there even when we do not want to go. It keeps us searching—keeps us going—keeps us listening and learning from one another even when we ourselves would not think to interrupt our busy lives for prayer. Then going to choir, praying the scriptures on which our souls and hearts and minds depend as a path to the True North of our lives, is never forgotten, never ignored. Without the monastic choir, for those for whom communal monasticism is their call, we would all be simply the latest version of the Lone Ranger, the cowpoke alone on her own horse in uncharted territory. For these, without help, without companionship, without mutual wisdom, without direction, without a spiritual home, the singular path could easily go dry, go to dust, go dull. The point is that having a spiritual community whose ways are clear and whose response is regular is essential. Coming to know the spiritual tradition, to wrestle with it together, to see it modeled, and so finally, over the years, to embrace it is one of the greatest gifts of community life.

Without a spiritual community to be called by, to be carried by when you yourself have no energy, no interest whatsoever in pursuing a spiritual regimen, you are adrift at sea. Without a compass, without a sextant, without the sight of the rising sun, you will find yourself in the darkest moments of life, in the darkness that comes with lack of support and loss of direction.

To be a monastic, then, means to absorb the tradition, to embrace that old, old Rule in all its dailiness, to immerse yourself in the wisdom and spiritual truth that monastics before you have passed on to you. Then there is no fear that you will become your own false guide, superficial witness to the deepest depths of the human heart, "the blind leading the blind." On the contrary. In community you are surrounded by "a cloud of witnesses" who show you the way.

It's finding a spiritual community that counts, that stretches you, that carries you on when you least feel like going on. If you're lucky, there is a monastic choir close to you that you can join, or if none is geographically available, gatherings like Monasteries of the Heart and other spiritual groups online offer daily horaria you can connect with there. Then, during those times when you cannot see the path before you, the choir will lift you up and take you to a place where, without them, you could not go but which you must discover if your own soul is to continue growing.

Just as private prayer focuses us largely on ourselves, communal prayer opens us up to the will of God for the world—of which we are meant to be factors. Then, in the end, we become the prayer we are immersed in—just in the face of injustice, merciful in the face of need, compassionate in the face of pain, and peaceful in the face of struggle.

9

BEAUTY

On the Invisible in the Visible

**The Rule of Benedict devotes an entire chapter titled
"The Artists of the Monastery." The relationship between
beauty and the spiritual life is a universal one.**

Monasticism is an established way of life that concentrates on the search for God. Art, the world treats, as the expression of personal truth. And yet, monasteries everywhere are centers, are veritable nuclei, of beauty: the grounds, the buildings themselves, the chapels, hallway galleries of religious art, the pottery and painting, the textile work, and the small publishing houses that produce special editions of cards and books and religious designs, all speak of a depth of soul beyond the ordinary.

One of the most surprising parts of monastic life in the modern world may well be its dedication to the arts, to the expression of passion and soul in a lifestyle that is too often seen as dour and lifeless. Why would monasteries make room for the arts in what is seen as a life of sacrifice? Why would anybody consider the arts a necessary stream of human pursuit rather than simply a glimpse of the matchless or a paean to culture or a glimpse of life unseen?

Why? Because the relationship between monastic life and art is palpable.

Since the time of the Greek philosophers, beauty has been counted among the ultimate values of the good life—equal even to values such as goodness and truth. In fact, the idea that the ascent of the mind to God is due to the beauty encountered in the physical world is an ancient one. And its corollary is so simple it's profound: Beauty itself is the key to the fullness of the spiritual life.

God is beauty, the theologians taught, and the universe is the irradiation of God's beauty. We see a face of God in the natural beauty of the world around us. Augustine was clear: "It is desire for the beautiful," he said, "that draws us to God." But if that's the case, the implication for the spiritual life stuns: To develop to our fullest, we must surround ourselves with beauty. As a result, monasticism cultivated the arts, and the arts expanded the spirit of monasticism.

Artists, most of whom were part of workshop teams that decorated cathedrals everywhere in Europe, were unnamed and unknown. Some entered the monastery and learned there that their artistry had a place, a voice, and a necessary role in religious life. The fifteenth-century painter Fra Angelico; the monk Gislebertus, trained by a master at the Abbey of Cluny in the twelfth century; and Abbot Suger, of the French Abbey of Saint Denis, were instrumental in developing new art styles while monks everywhere illuminated by hand Bibles that became the artwork of the monasteries.

Secular artists followed monastic communities from one region to another to become part of the monastic movement that spurred the building of the great cathedrals all over Europe. Rather than suppress art, as religious traditions in the name of spiritual detachment from sensuality began to do centuries later, early monasticism saw great art as an aspect of spiritual development. These monastics learned, too, that they had a moral obligation to see that their art was affordable, was a kind of gift to those who could not pay the going price for it.

The reasoning is clear: Both artists and monastics devote themselves to seeking God. Since art reflects the beauty of creativity, art makes the beauty of God the Creator present. Then beauty becomes a tool of spiritual development, a necessary part of our ascent to God, another incarnation, another revelation of God among us.

Visual expression, great chant, polyphony, architecture, glasswork, poetry, and writing were all meant to engage the whole of a person. They raised the soul to mystical height. The great vaulted ceilings of these cathedrals called down immensity upon us. The intensely bright glass in the soaring stained-glass windows above the nave brought God's brightness into our dusk. The massive stonework, the choral music, the haunting chants lifted the mystical soul up to heaven. New churches with their ever higher spires and mythical gargoyles and statues pointing to eternal holiness became the living parts of the ponderous architecture by which medieval cathedrals and monasteries wrenched souls up out of the dregs of life to the anterooms of heaven.

Integrating the Practice

Without the arts—architecture, sculpture, painting, literature, music, performance, and film—the soul dries up, the world goes dark. Then plastics and faux leather and pressed wood and the whole gamut of bogus, fabricated, or counterfeit attempts to persuade you that the unreal is real turn the world upside down. The ability to reproduce becomes more important than the inspiration or creativity of an original form or a unique rendition of an idea. Reproduction becomes more important than originality. And your life takes on more of the unreal than the real.

"Beauty in things," the philosopher David Hume writes, "exists in the mind which contemplates them." It is the artist who brings the soul to see the visible in the invisible. It is art that is the lifeline of contemplation.

In our own time, in a world of assembly lines and paint-by-numbers, beauty stopped being central to a technological world. Function became the driving engine of society. The world settled down to the repetition of sameness, the reduction of the original to the level of the mundane. The statues of David in plastic and the plethora of great historic figures in soap carvings, the consignment of people to high-rise apartment buildings, one after the other of them the same, have hastened the death of the imagination. We start to die inside ourselves and never even know it. We cease to understand our nature as spiritual beings because there is nothing in the environment either to challenge our assumptions or to lift our hearts and minds, nothing to stir our souls to life again and newly again.

It is beauty, in other words, that enables us to rise above the sordid in life and so to transform life from the inside out, to give it meaning, to give it feeling, to give it insight, to give it a vision of a better world. To this day monasticism reminds us that art stretches us beyond the sleazy, the superficial, the fake, the false, and the gaudy. Beauty transports us. It refuses to be dull. It gives life to the lifeless—the hopeless—and changes the spiritual life from an experience of rules to an expression of awe.

Artists give us new ways to see the unseeable, but it is monasticism that exists in pursuit of the beauty of the invisible God. It is the monastic heart in us, therefore, which, committed to seeking God, must cultivate the artistic spirit, nurture it, be keepers of it, re-create it. Art cleanses our senses of the mundane. It awakens us to see more than things, and beyond things to new insights about life, about new feelings, about a new sense of transcendence.

It is up to you and me, then, to make art a sacrament of modern life. Art in the hands of an artist makes our homes, our small apartments, our minds centers of the beauty we pursue through the galleries of life.

Make your soul a seeker of the arts and your environment a holy site that rejects the tawdry, the artificial, and the vulgar.

If the question is whether it is possible to have a real spiritual life without a sense of beauty, the answer of an ancient and anonymous poet is a simple one: "When you have only two pennies left in the world, buy a loaf of bread with one and a lily with the other."

Both artists and monastics devote themselves to seeking God. Since art reflects the beauty of creativity, art makes the beauty of God the Creator present. Then beauty becomes a tool of spiritual development, a necessary part of our ascent to God, another incarnation, another revelation of God among us.

10

SILENCE

On Inner Quietude

The notion that silence is a fundamental element of the
spiritual life is one of the most ancient concepts in religion.
Silence will differ from one community to another in matters
of length, place, rigor, or ritual to meet the local situation.
But no monastic community in any tradition lives without it.
It is in silence that the spiritual life grows.

At the end of the day—after supper, perhaps, or after evening
prayer, or at a customary time—in monastic communities
everywhere, silence descends on the monastery. Total silence en-
gulfs the group until sometime the next morning. Unusual? On
the contrary. Silence has been an underlying element of spiritual
development in every monastic community of every great spiritual tradition for over five thousand years.

I remember the feelings of both security and social separation
that the silence brought to me in my first months of transition
from the noise of the streets to the soundlessness of the tiled halls
of the monastery. It affected me so deeply when I was a young
novice. The same sisters who had walked the halls all day still
walked them at night, on their way to study or finish preparations
for the next day, but their steps were even softer, their pace was

slower, their presence near me felt almost ghostlike. We had become a different place, a more modulated group, a more centered band of people than the ones who had moved quickly and efficiently only minutes before.

Silence was the one part of monastic life that was completely distinct from anything I had known outside the monastery. Here the entire community simply wafted away, singly, softly, silently. No good-night rituals. No last-minute shared projects. No expectations of group work. You could almost hear a communal sigh of relief and the hearts around you relax as the quiet set in. We were individuals now, on our own, inside ourselves, ruminating.

Suddenly I began to be aware of all the teachings about silence that I'd heard over the years but had given very little attention to, however profound they had seemed. Later, I began to realize they were everywhere. The seventeenth-century mathematician-theologian Blaise Pascal wrote of silence, "All a person's miseries derive from not being able to sit in a quiet room alone." Even Albert Einstein said, "The monotony and solitude of a quiet life stimulates the creative mind."

Every tradition conceives of silence as "the Gateway to God," the entrée to spiritual wisdom, the beginning of interior peace, the first step to self-control. Silence, the masters repeat, is the first step to wisdom, the door to self-awareness. Silence, the monastics come to realize, is the link that connects us to the Divine. However we define the Ultimate, only silence will take us there. It is in the very act of carving out twenty minutes a day to sit in silence—as we do—that silence begins to shape us: First, our heartbeat slows a bit. Then, our mind sinks into a sense of oneness with life.

Silence in all its forms and all its times will change us. Most of all, if we cultivate it, it will put down roots in our souls and engender peace in our lives. It will give us a healthy way to deal with the ideas that occupy and often irritate the depths of us. It will grow us beyond our uncertainties and into the presence of God. Simply by centering us, by calming us, by settling us—our bodies, our eyes, our minds—silence captures the soul. Silence will simply lead us down, down, down into the center of the self, to spiritual interiority, to a life of meaning and freedom from fear.

Then we will "grow to full stature." We will become spiritual people in pursuit of the productive kind of silence whose voice resounds in us now. Concentration on the empty counterclaims of life—its fruitless promises—and contemplation of the Word will, together, bring us to the stilled fullness of our selves. Then restlessness ceases, agitation quiets, and the groundless grasping for the baubles of life dies away. The clamoring for the kind of moreness that exhausts our energy evaporates, and our souls come to rest in the heart of calm.

No amount of time spent skimming over the shallows of life while we go superficially through the rituals of religion but ignore its marrow can ever bring us to the wholeness of ourselves. Only by immersing ourselves softly, quietly, placidly in the silence that centers us in the essence of life can we ever come to live truth to the core, life to the full.

Integrating the Practice

The modern world has begun to understand the effects of noise, but has done little to examine the effects of silence, the only real antidote we have to the constant rattle and roar, blaring and shouting of contemporary life. And yet, there is in our midst a tradition whose embrace of silence marks its very character and gift.

Down in the depths of silence, distant from the crowds, alone with yourself, your life lays itself bare before you, begging to be really seen. All the tensions swim to the surface noiselessly, though you have spent weeks—sometimes years—trying to ignore the need to deal with them: to have the conversations, to see the people you do not want to see, to do the new work, to confront difficulties, or to summon up the courage to start over. You face the call of silence to begin again, to become the kind of person you really want to be. It's all there—but only silence can walk you through it to the end.

Silence comes to you with very clear gifts, which often do not feel like gifts at first glance. It challenges you. If you are faithful to it and true to yourself, it can be the moment when you begin to evolve beyond your secrets to the truths about yourself that are for yourself alone to resolve. Able to mull over all the old prescriptions about how to live that came from someone else's bag of internalized commandments, you can now choose for yourself which to keep—and which not. You can blot out the noises of life that rattle you, and distract you, and blur your ideas about living the life you want. Most of all, you can sit soundlessly until you come to know who you really are—who you really want to be.

Silence gives you the opportunity to do things thoughtfully. To proceed seriously. To speak up bravely. You can listen for the voice of God within you calling you to the more of life that you have smothered for so long that the voice has become barely audible. You can learn, as well, to listen to others—to the world, the family, the friends, the lovers of life around you—and learn from their insights in addition to your own.

No doubt about it, silence is the beginning of wisdom as it sorts and casts out, rethinks and reclaims, plans and proceeds so that you can become your true self. As someone once wrote, "A meaningful silence is always better than meaningless words."

There is no substitute for silence in the spiritual life. There is no substitute for the need to wrestle with your demons and your angels, as Jacob did, to find the path, the light, and the spiritual strength it will take to do what must be done. As the Islamic poet Rumi wrote, "Listen to silence; it has much to say."

Yes, silence separates you from all the masks and distractions of life. It rips the veil from the postures and arguments you have clung to as justification for your social sins. And yet, ironically, only silence can bring you to the union of the self with the spirit within you that makes life true, makes life authentic, makes life worth living.

It is in the very act of carving out twenty minutes a day to sit in silence that silence begins to shape us: First, our heartbeat slows a bit. Then, our mind sinks into a sense of oneness with life.

11

LECTIO

On Reading Between the Lines

Lectio, or lectio divina, is the art of sacred reading. It is the practice of reading scripture and holy books with conscious reflection on ideas that lead to understanding, to spiritual growth, to a new level of spiritual maturity, and to a new depth of union with God.

Two stories explain lectio divina best, I think. The first is a child's reaction to the Christmas story about the Flight into Egypt and the angel's direction to Joseph. "To escape King Herod," the father intoned with a certain amount of drama, "take the baby and Mary and flee into Egypt." When the story was over, the little boy, wonderstruck, said breathlessly, "What happened to the flea?" And the parents, puzzled, said, "What flea?" And the little boy said, "The one the man was told to take with the baby and Mary and flea into Egypt."

We laugh at the child's confusion, but I can't help but wonder how many of us read scripture and holy books for years without understanding what they're really saying. Or worse, without even beginning to grapple with the ideas they present for us to live by and keep.

The second story confronts adults with an even more significant issue. "Rabbi," the disciple said, "have you really gone through the entire Torah?" And the rabbi answered, "My friend, the question is not Have you gone through the Torah? The question is Has the Torah gone through you?"

Which is exactly where lectio divina comes in. Sacred reading is what stops us from dashing through spiritual ideas without stopping to consider exactly what they mean to us today. Or actually meant to anybody—even in the times when they were first read. In fact, sacred reading is not an exercise in reading the greatest number of holy books we can get our hands on. On the contrary, sacred reading is about prodding thought, not finishing pages. It is meant to begin a long and deliberate conversation with God about what it means to be alive, to be holy, to be "in the Spirit," to be a disciple—now and here.

Lectio divina is meant to encourage one to think. To grapple with a holy idea until its depth and call reshape our souls. To get it, as the Chinese proverb says, a drop at a time until it wears away our hard-heartedness like water dripping on a rock. Then, when we have scraped off the outer layer of an old and, we thought, hackneyed idea, we see it afresh and it shows us the way to a new dimension of the spiritual life.

Lectio, then, is the practice of extracting from every sentence, every phrase, every word of a psalm or Gospel passage, its meaning for the reader at this time, in this age. It is a journey into the cave of the heart. This reading becomes a dialogue among writer, reader, and the spirit of God within us. It gives us insight, understanding, a new spirit, the flowering of the soul. Best of all, lectio, every novice knows, is a *process,* not simply an interesting thought.

There are five levels of lectio divina:

1. Reading a text
2. Praying to understand it
3. Questioning oneself
4. Reflecting on the text
5. Making decisions about one's life

Each of these steps, like a spiral staircase, takes us down more and more into the text, into the concepts, into its meaning for me now, and for my spiritual development always.

Sacred reading is the beginning of a conversation with God. Without it, how do we "grow" on through life?

Integrating the Practice

Lectio divina is the monastic entry to contemplation. It puts you in touch with the mind of God. Lectio takes you beyond spiritual childhood to spiritual maturity, turning over the soil of your soul to see what's really underneath: Is it complacency, disinterest, self-satisfaction, fear? What is it inside of you that makes life's challenges so difficult for you?

Lectio opens your mind and your heart to new ways, holier ways, more just and peaceful ways of being in the world.

The process is a simple but profound one.

First, perhaps you are reading a text from the Bible. Or from a book of spiritual writers or possibly from a poem or a prayer.

Maybe you're reading a book that calls for faith. So what exactly is faith? you begin to wonder. And what does it demand of me here and now? Do those things call for faith in Jesus or for conformity to the man-made rules of the Church? You read the words over and over, looking for some resolution of your own position on the subject.

Second, you stop and pray for insight about this. You ask God to help you live with the doubts you don't know how to resolve. Then this struggle with the idea of faith begins a long conversation with God that you revisit often.

Third, you begin to think deeply, seriously, profoundly about the difference between faith and mere compliance with a system. You think of Jesus, who was also having trouble with a system that was failing the tradition of the prophets. You look for your own place at the bar of the Gospel, seeking the just, the wise, the godly answer.

Fourth, you contemplate the great commitments of Jesus and compare your own depth of commitments. Do you really commit to anything—or just talk about it? You ask for the courage to be Jesus in this place and this question and this time.

Fifth, you ask yourself what you can do to resolve this struggle in your own life right now—maybe not fully or comprehensively, but at least one degree more than you'd know how to do otherwise.

And then, you begin another reading. And you'll stop where something stops you, and start again to shape and reshape your growing soul.

Clearly, lectio is the growth process of prayer. It is not recitation of a formula; it is confrontation with the self. It is the next step to maturity of soul. Lectio divina is more than simply saying a set of prayers. In lectio you live into the prayers, the psalms, the parables. You accept the challenge of your growing. Then the rabbi's answer is obvious and easy. Lectio asks you, too: Are you simply going through the Gospel or is the Gospel going through you? Differently. With great impact. For the sake of the world?

Sacred reading is about prodding thought, not finishing pages. It is meant to begin a long and deliberate conversation with God about what it means to be alive, to be holy, to be "in the Spirit," to be a disciple—now and here. Lectio divina is meant to prod thought. To grapple with a holy idea until its depth and call reshape our souls.

12

CLOISTER

On Sacred Space

In modern usage, *cloister* means monastery life itself, as in
"She went to the cloister." In early Benedictine monastic life,
however, the cloister was a quadrangular inner garden meant
to facilitate the quality of monastic life—to allow for
the sacred space that a monastic life requires.

Early monasticism outgrew its pioneer character quickly. After
the fall of Rome, in 476, the civil organization that had been
Rome's genius crumbled and died. Under pressure from immigrant tribes threatening the borders, and bereft of the prestigious
Roman legions that once guarded them, the government of Rome
was weak, social control had withered, and local princes vied in-
cessantly for land, wealth, and power. The peasants and serfs, their
farms burning or looted thanks to the constant upheaval of unending local wars, left the land to wander the open roads for food
and safety.

Only one thing emerged to bring order and stability to an
empire in chaos—the newly developing Benedictine communities and their monastic structures: work, prayer, community harmony, and obedience to a spiritual authority. They were creating
a new way of life, a new type of social organization, and a new way

of living together that brought the return of civil order, education, and vision to a people without a clear center, a firm rudder,
a stable future.

The monasteries, often endowed by wealthy patrons, developed public hospices, created educational centers, established
civil regions, and renewed a system of agriculture long abandoned
by the now unemployed peasants who once farmed these ravaged
lands. In fact, the monasteries grew quickly into manorial sites
rather than isolated communities. Serfs and lay crafters and laborers simply moved onto property surrounding the abbeys and prio-
ries where monks taught them to read and to farm. Monasteries
became civil settlements with the monastics as teachers, doctors,
judges, and keepers of a kind of monastic society. It was a great
and noble demonstration of what ordinary life lived extraordinarily well can do for a society.

But there was another aspect of it as well. A very personal one.

As the monasteries grew and expanded their presence, they
began to melt into the fabric of the larger community. Then they
began to realize that if things didn't change, the communities, the
monastics themselves, would lose their new identity and the lifestyle that went with it. And the lifestyle that went with it would
simply disappear as a distinct identity. They would find themselves drawn back into the larger world. Their boundaries were
being overrun, their private lives encroached upon. They began to
be more and more enveloped by the secular society that now lived
and worked on monastery property. Their new world built inside
of the old would be gone. This was a moment for great decisions.

So what did those monastics do? They built for themselves
what has become the distinguishing sign of monastic architecture:
the cloister.

Surrounded by the chapel on the east side, the refectory across
from it, the kitchen across the garden, and the chapter/assembly

room on the other side, they built an open space in the midst of a monastic quadrangle and surrounded it with an open walkway under a slanted roof. It was private space, quiet space, that connected all four major parts of the square with its cruciform paths. There, on the cloister walk, monastics met, meditated, read the scriptures, prayed, studied, and wrote. Uninterrupted. Alone. With great concentration. And as a result, as involved as they all were with the peasants around them, monasticism—the avowed search for "the one thing Important, God"—continued to grow, committed to its ideals as the sign of another way of life. Even today.

Integrating the Practice

You have known times when the difficulty of life is not so much the pressure of your work, or the needs of the children, or the eternal presence of neighbors and family; it's the inability to protect yourself from all of it. For just a bit. An hour, maybe. A morning, perhaps. Just some time where you can sit and answer some mail without being interrupted. Or make big decisions about the cost of new furniture or the possibility of taking a new job. Or maybe just enough time to sit and do some lectio of your own, or finally have the book club in.

But the time never comes because the need for that kind of time is forever perpetual: You go from a small town to a large city and pretty soon you never see the cousins again. You leave the suburb, go back to school, and become a nurse. Great, but you also never know again what it's like to walk home from work, play with the kids, and go out to an early movie together. You start a small business that succeeds, and pretty soon you have a chain of them and all the paperwork and oversight and competition that implies. You get a job in the office of the large corporation and before you know it you're traveling two weeks out of every month to help all the branch offices.

They're all good things that take you from the good thing that created you and now leave you with astounding questions. Questions that change the very nature of life, as in, How much of a mortgage is too much? And once started down that road, how do I get off it?

Or worse, What do I do when my marriage begins to turn gray? Get a divorce? Quit the job that's tearing us apart? Try to revive our union by refusing the next promotion? What can we possibly do to preserve what we set out to do, to be, to live a glorious family life?

It's then that cloister—the ability to make your life private in ways the early monastics did—cries out for resolution. You need enough space to get personal work done free from outside pressures. And yet at the same time, you have to keep in touch with the work and the people who need you there.

If cloister was needed by the early Middle Ages, it may be even more important, more meaningful in our day. Right now. In this time—when you're beginning to work from home and take care of the kids, walk the dog, and let the electrician in to rewire the electric heater—and all those things at once. In fact, maybe it's most of all in this time that the meaning and value of cloister are clear and are essential parts of the spiritual life. Anybody's spiritual life, everybody's spiritual life.

Who, in this culture of so many demands, so many questions, so many needs, does not feel consumed by it all? Who of us is not in danger of losing what we must maintain—if we are to save our marriages, raise our children lovingly, and become the most developed people we can possibly be—if we find ourselves too swamped to think? If we do not find someplace beautiful enough, peaceful enough to think it all through carefully and quietly, what will be left of our personalities, our goodwill, our energy to give away?

Indeed, the cloister is where you go to save yourself for the sake of the other. The real question for the monastic heart everywhere is, Where is your cloister? In the car as you commute to work? In the glassed-in porch where the flowers bloom? In the little closet you've made your home office? How often do you go there to refresh your own soul, to rest your own gifts? If not often enough, don't worry about what you need to do for others. It is far too late for that. It's what you do for yourself that will be most helpful to them as well.

It's then that cloister—the ability to make our lives private in ways the early monastics did—cries out for resolution. We need enough space to get personal work done free from outside pressures.

13

THE MONASTIC CELL

On Privacy

Monastics do not sleep the way they spend most of the rest of community life, in groups. Unless the group has outgrown the facilities, members sleep in individual "cells," from *celle,* the French word for hermitage or private space.

When I entered the monastery, the building did not have private rooms enough for every younger sister to have a private cell. Instead, we lived in dormitories. Older sisters were given private rooms as long as they were available. But it took almost twenty years before the community was able to enlarge the monastery to the point that every sister could have a private bedroom, could have enough space for a bed, a chair, and a small dresser.

In early centuries, family members often slept in one room—even in the same bed. In the Rule of Benedict, there is a chapter titled "The Sleeping Arrangements of Monastics." But there was nothing penitential or sacrificial about it. In religious communities it was normal for the size of the monastery itself to dictate the use of its rooms. As the centuries went by, the culture of monastic sleeping arrangements changed with the culture around the monasteries. By our day and age, no one doubted that having a private cell was not only desirable but necessary.

Space, like silence, is recognized in the Rule of Benedict as a vital part of spiritual development. Yes, community is the goal of monasticism, but every monastic tradition—Hinduism and its ashrams, Orthodox Christianity and its poustinias, Western Christianity and its hermitages—allowed for personal space at the same time as monastics saw community as their goal.

But why?

In the first place, lectio calls for contemplation. But where? Where is it possible for anyone, let alone a vowed monastic, to concentrate on reflection in the midst of a moving system? In the modern world, which brings email, public address announcements, TV programs, and earbuds, privacy and quiet are as essential to human and spiritual development as breathing. Space and time and privacy are eternally recurring issues in modern society. As cities, not farms, took over the developing world, space and privacy became social issues as well as personal ones.

No, no one needs perfect silence. Actually, there is no such thing. But everyone does need the opportunity to have a door between herself and the rest of the world. At least once a day. Even in a monastery. All of the demands of the world seep in, even into a monastic atmosphere. Some may need to concentrate on work or study or relaxation, while others may need space and quiet at the same time.

The door between me and the world is the door to my spiritual development, and that means both dimensions of it. The first door opens into my ministry. That one totally empties me of my personal self and shifts my attention to all the needs around me. The second door, on the other hand, calls me to sink into the kind of contemplation that can stretch my soul, open my heart, change my entire life. If I can only find the time it takes to immerse myself in the spiritual struggle of it all. If I can begin to see the light on a new path. If there is only the space I need to think it through.

The monastic cell gives me the privacy I need to continue what lectio has prompted in me: the need to recognize, to reshape what is going on within my soul right now. To discover what it is that is agitating me, preoccupying me, distracting me, holding me back from becoming the rest of who I am meant to be.

The questions that seep up through lectio are legion: Am I being drawn to another kind of life? Is this the spirit of God prompting me to stretch myself a bit more? Should I just quit this thing? Or is this desire to quit what I am doing in midair the very epitome of my self-centeredness, my unwillingness to pour myself out one more day of my life for anyone else but myself? The answers are just as complex as the questions: Maybe it is time for me to move on? But how will I know? Where is the spirit most settled, most active, most alive in me?

It's when I'm most disturbed by the anxiety that won't go away or the frustration that comes from unresolved differences or obstructions or personal hurts that I need privacy most. It's then that everything I thought I had learned in prayer and reflection is tested by stress. When I think I am finally beginning to ignore the little agitations of life, I need the privacy to allow the reactions and rage of the moment to burn off without harming anyone, me or my nemesis at the time. Privacy gives me the space to face myself, to challenge me to become my best self.

These are great, demanding impulses. They take time to work through. They need clear-minded attention or I may stumble into exactly what I cannot do, just for the sake of doing something else.

Integrating the Practice

Concentration is the key to human balance. Contemplation of the will of God—what it is; what, specifically, you hear it saying to you at this moment—is the ground of the spiritual life. Spirituality is not a series of practices—of praying so many prayers, of spending so much time in church, of giving money or time to charity, as important as those things may be. Spirituality is the conscious turning of the mind and the spirit to God that softens the edges of the heart, that increases your understanding and enlightens your heart before you manage to make the small things in life bigger than they ought to be.

For that experience of the spiritual life, monastics knew that we each need a cell, a simple little place, with a small shrine, maybe—something to keep our attention on God present within us rather than on the irritations of the day. You must learn to sit in a calming place, with a bit of incense, perhaps, or the soft aroma of a cinnamon candle, the Bible in hand and maybe a bit of chant playing to help one listen for the promptings of the Spirit in one's soul. There, day after day, we begin to slip into silence. We learn to listen within for what the Spirit is saying about all these things in today's Gospel. And we relax; we begin to see life in terms of the size of the grain of sand that is irritating our hearts—small? minuscule? invisible?—and grow beyond it.

The movement into privacy enables me to seek real-time answers to the great questions of life: what I myself, for instance, should be doing to change people's attitudes about immigrants, about my relationships with my own relatives, about what to do with the anger that is eating me away inside. Contemplation is the answer to the question What does God want of me right now, here, in this situation? And why am I afraid of it? Why am I resisting it? Why am I finding this journey into the Spirit in me so difficult? What exactly do I believe? And what can I do to bring my spirit back to life?

The cell is about having a place where everything in your heart, all the thorns in your soul, can be worked through, over and over again if necessary, while you go on with your lectio divina until the answers finally emerge. The cell should be a private place, where others do not intrude to plan programs or watch a movie or start conversations. Your cell belongs to God and you. God is always there. If you are faithful, you will be there, too, one day.

Everyone needs the opportunity to close a door between herself and the rest of the world. At least once a day.

14

METANOIA

On Growth

**Conversion of life is the process of deep-seated psychological
and spiritual transformation after which a person's view of life
and behavior are permanently and profoundly altered. It is
one of the three vows specific to the Benedictine tradition.**

I have a friend, the son of a very successful and admired socially
active pastor in the United States. The problem was that he was
a PK—a preacher's kid—who had apparently had all the preach-
ing he could take. When it came time for him to decide what he
would do with his life, he got on a motorcycle and left. Just riding
across the country as fast as he could go.

He went nowhere and everywhere. For two years, he raced
from bar to bar, cheap motel to cheap motel, woman after woman,
and blackjack table after blackjack table until it happened: He
simply broke down one night—much like scripture's Prodigal
Son. When he woke up two days later, sober and shaken—all the
years of his good life burned into the fiber of his mind—he said
to himself, "What in God's name am I doing here?" Then he got
back on his motorcycle and rode for three straight days to get
home to his Prodigal Father.

He finally decided to go to the seminary—no pressure whatsoever from his father—but realized that missionary work was more suited to his personality and talents than pastoring a congregation. So he and his equally committed priest-wife developed one of the first video sets of religious programs in the United States. They took small-town ministry to the highest levels of visual communication and brought ministers everywhere the resources they need to be the kinds of good pastors they so much want to be.

That type of change, his total change, is metanoia. That's conversion of life.

Psychologists later began to call a struggle like that an identity crisis. Something cataclysmic. Something unacceptable. But that makes it sound very rare, when, as a matter of fact, it is a very, very common dimension of spiritual development. Most of us go through such a change on some level. No, not generally on a motorcycle or in a chain of cheap hotels and high-rolling casinos. But always to the very edge of something; always to the point of real decision. As in, I can go on drinking or I can get dried out. I can continue to risk my marriage or I can recommit. I can simply let the decay of the world start with me and wonder someday how and why it happened or I can give myself to something that changes my little piece of the world for the better.

Instead, most of us deal with our moments of truth at very pedestrian levels. Meaning, we make a mistake and we lie about it. Until years later. Then the strain of it sours our personalities and drains our energy and leaves us spiritually limp and dried out without a clue what to do next. It just ruminates inside of us. It becomes our great, haunting secret.

We know that something's wrong with us, with our lives, but we don't know what. We at least know that life could be, should be, much better than it is. If we're lucky, we find a good friend, a good counselor, a good spiritual director—the Rule of Benedict and some form of lectio divina—and stop in our tracks to look life over. Then, finally, begins our confrontation with the self and our conversation with God.

Lectio divina, we know now, is not the process of simply reading holy books. It is the process of grappling with them, wrestling the great ideas to the ground of our souls until we finally rise out of the tomb of the self a new person. A genuine person who has put down all the public scripts of success—"butcher, baker, candlestick maker," someone to be reckoned with—and confesses to themselves how none of it is real.

Then we are ready to be ourselves. Then life takes on newness again. Then tomorrow is a day to be shaped, not hidden, not a secret we cannot tell for fear of being seen for who and what we really are. Metanoia is the great moment of spiritual—and, if truth be told, of social and public and holy—liberation from the burden of pretending to be what we are not. Now we can never be afraid again to be seen for what we were—and what we have become.

Integrating the Practice

Metanoia, conversion of life, calls you to see yourself as you are, not as you want other people to see you. Once you put down the mask, once you stop pretending to yourself as well as others that you are what you may seem, you are on the road to new life. You can make peace with the old enemy now; you can heal the family; you can pay the bills. You can sell the big house, give up the huge mortgage, and begin to live at your level in all its liberating simplicity. And not be ashamed of it.

You can stop competing for the world's attention. You can confess the great lies. You can put down your weapons of defensiveness, condemnation of others, character assassination, divisiveness, and all your homegrown dogmatism that has separated you from so many. But first you must recognize these things and forswear them. Once you confess these things at least to yourself, once you understand the harm you have done to others, as well as to yourself, you are on the verge of becoming the person you are meant to be.

Then the pain you have unknowingly inflicted on yourself—the tension that comes with bitterness, the anxiety that comes with public rejection, the fear that comes with living the charade which once consumed you—evaporates. You begin to see life differently. You become better, kinder, softer with others—and feel safer yourself now that you're not hiding anymore.

This is metanoia. The transformation of the self. The change of heart is accomplished now. You have become your truer self. The sting of contrition may last for a while, regret certainly may set in as you make your way through the long journey of reuniting with the people you've hurt and correcting the stories you've told.

Self-awareness is the basis of the cleansing process, and it does not entirely depend on your being able to reconcile with those you've hurt or abandoned or besmirched. It really depends on your admission to yourself of what you did and why you did it and what it did to other people. Even more, you face what it did to your own growth and happiness, your own integrity and self-development. You look back and realize what your choices did to life as you know it now. And most of all, you commit to what you will do no more, make excuses for no more, hide from no more.

And you become new again.

The psychologists William James and Carl Jung, who launched this great spiritual-psychological work of inner healing, knew that though the process is intense, the self-surrender releases your energy of soul, your zest for life, all over again. Most certain of all, what Kazimierz Dąbrowski calls positive disintegration—this dis-

mantling of the old, false self so that the real, true self can
emerge—is the beginning of happiness.

Metanoia—conversion of life—is not penitential or destructive. It lifts the weight off your soul. It gives you back to yourself.
It is a fundamental change, a transformative change of heart that
will lead you to a new way of being alive. A wholesome way. An
honest way. A brave way. All that it requires is that you start the
dismantling yourself.

**Once we put down the masks, once we stop pretending to our-
selves as well as others that we are not what we may seem, we
are on the road to new life.**

15

FUGA MUNDI

On Living in the World or Not

Fuga mundi, to flee the world, is one of the oldest—and has been one of the most troublesome—of monastic concepts. It has been a shifting notion for centuries. The question of a Christian's relationship with the world affects the very nature of religious life and the spirituality that underlies it.

So what's the answer? Should Christians be *in* the world but not *of* the world?

When the Roman emperor Constantine legalized Christianity in the fourth century, the faith suddenly found itself in the middle of a new and even more difficult question than persecution had presented. How should Christians deal with this new relationship: separate from a clearly sin-ridden world, flee the world to save their souls, or engage with the world in order to reshape it? In one way or another, those options have plagued religious life ever since.

Once Constantine and Theodosius declared Christianity, small and undeveloped as it was, to be the state religion of the empire, religion became a relatively pedestrian matter. People eased into daily life at greater or lesser degrees of intensity. The most avid of the Christian community argued that the civil identification of Romans with Christianity actually weakened Christianity's pristine energy rather than strengthening the Jesus story. Like the ascetics before them, this group chose to flee the city for the austere and simple life of the desert. In their minds, doing battle with Satan in the desert, rather than identifying with the easy life in a sinful world, promised salvation. Anything else was not real Christianity. It was, at best, a sinful compromise.

From the Greek philosophers on, the relationship between matter and spirit was the great spiritual question of the time. Only the Spirit was holy, some argued, and they rejected matter as the stuff of evil, delusion, the enemy of the soul. The Church rejected that view as heretical. After all, God, who created us, also created matter. How could that matter be evil in and of itself?

So these Christian "monastics of the desert" did not revolt against the Constantinian decree of Christian legitimacy or condemn those who approved of it or ignore those for whom it had little meaning. They simply took it upon themselves to become new kinds of standard-bearers of the faith, to practice it in its more pristine and compelling ways, and eventually found themselves functioning as spiritual directors to those who stayed in the cities but looked to the communities of Christians in the desert for spiritual guidance. It was a clear geographical fuga mundi, a flight from one world to another in order to gain salvation. In this definition, it set a line of demarcation that has marked every century since, this one included.

The writings of that early period abound. The question lingers still but now in different ways. What does "flee the world" mean now to us? Should we flee the world God made? How is it possible in this century to separate from others in the name of religion? And is doing things like that religious at all? Even more important: Is religion all about creeds and canons? Or is religion all about the individual soul's relationship to God? Whomever we call God. We are, after all, in the world. We really cannot flee it. But we can address its needs, and we can, like Jesus, live *in* it but not *of* it.

To reject the world is to reject creation, reject the model of the Jesus whose life in the world was world-changing, reject the blessings of life in the world as well as its evils. The situation is clear: It is possible to be *too* spiritual if rejection of the work of God is your idea of being spiritual.

If nothing else, this kind of thinking diminishes the value of creation. It introduces a kind of theology of domination, which gives humans the right to destroy, pollute, and deny our dependence on the rest of life. It opens us up to cruelty to animals, to the servitude of human beings that we call less human than we are. It denies us all the joy of living in a glorious creation and runs the danger of making our love for the things of earth nothing more than a new kind of idol. We separate ourselves from all responsibility for the care of creation. We put in its spiritual place a false kind of detachment that teaches that to be fully God's we must give up all the other gifts God has given us.

Integrating the Practice

Clearly, confusion like this—Is it holier to leave the world for fear of being compromised by it than to stay in it and serve it?—would affect monasticism. As the earliest of religious orders in the sixth century, monasticism fell prey to the earliest answers of the earliest debates on it. But so did every religious order after them, from the twelfth century on.

The questions were legion: Should monks and nuns be allowed to leave their monasteries? Should the laity mix with ministers and congregations of other denominations? Should intermarriage between even Christian sects be permitted? Should girls, allegedly more irrational and fragile than men, be allowed to function in the public arena, where evil plied its way? Should Christians go as missionaries to non-Christian peoples and, if so, to do what? All those kinds of questions flow from whether we believe that we can be saved from anything that is not us and our kind only by "fleeing from the world."

In fact, only in our own time, at Vatican Council II, 1962 through 1965, did the Council documents declare, in *Lumen Gentium:* "Let no one think that their consecrated way of life alienates religious from others or makes them useless for human society."

Monastics are not meant to flee the world. Rather, you and I resist the spirit of the world that is violent—oppressive of women, blind to injustice, enslaving of the working poor. Together we resist the spirits of greed, of sexism, of racism, of discrimination that enables the wealthy of the world to get even wealthier at the expense of those upon whose shoulders the work of the world with its unjust wages falls. We resist the spirit of a world that declares the life of the globe a resource rather than a responsibility. We resist the brutal and uncaring regard for animals, their death and exploitation by the hundreds of thousands, the abandonment of children to starvation, unresolved epidemics, lack of education, and bestial housing in the barrios of the world. We resist the institutionalizing of poverty while the wealthy on the hills above the poor look down and do nothing about any of it.

Monasticism seeks one thing: the will of God for this world. It does not flee the world; it refuses to allow the great questions of life and the world to be silenced, to be ignored, to be overlooked, to be discounted.

You and I have so much to learn. Monastics have addressed

the needs of every age or they could not have existed for over fifteen hundred years. They obviously weren't fleeing from anything—except evil itself! And, like them, neither must we.

Monasticism seeks one thing: the will of God for this world. It does not flee the world. It refuses to allow the great questions of life and the world to be silenced, to be ignored, to be overlooked, to be discounted.

16

~

COMMUNITY

On Spiritual Companionship

**Community is the coming together of unrelated people for
the sake of a particular vision or goal.**

Everybody everywhere exists in some kind of community. Few
people, if any, are entirely removed from the lives of those
around them. And few fail to interact with the community of
ideas in which they exist: some economically, others socially, most
racially or nationally, many spiritually.

At the same time, however, "community" exists in different
degrees. The first is a union of minds, meaning that we share common ideas. Intentional groups that work together create some
kind of defined social entity. These are people who share a union
of hearts, meaning they share common feelings about people, the
world, a particular situation. Those who share a union of souls
hold a common creed or spiritual practices for the sake of their
personal spiritual development.

At an even deeper level, some people, like monastics, decide to
live their lives together, for the sake of supporting one another
physically as well as spiritually as we seek the common good, the
vision of God for this continually developing Garden of Paradise.

Benedict of Nursia, for instance, the founder of cenobitic

monasticism—or monasticism lived in community—reminds us in the Prologue to his Rule that the preeminent call of the Christian life is to follow the will of God. There are, he says, four kinds of monks: cenobites, hermits, sarabaites, and gyrovagues. All of them claim to be religious figures. All of them live that life differently.

Cenobites, Benedict says, live in community under the Rule and Abbots and Abbesses. This type, he says, commit themselves to a single vision of life and accept a spiritual leader to guide their seeking. The second type, he teaches, are hermits, who, long trained by spiritual mentors, eventually leave the group to live alone and devote themselves to a prayerful and ascetical life. They are beacons to many. The third type of monastics Benedict describes are sarabaites—monks, he says, who go from place to place, without fixed residence or leadership, and rely on other people to support them as they go. And fourth are the gyrovagues, who roam from place to place, who never settle down, but who live off the hospitality of others. They are soft souls posturing as spiritually strong. They are not the real thing, he says. They have no discipline, no spiritual depth.

Then Benedict sends a message that is as important today as it was then: Holiness is not a claim we make; it is a way of life like any other. It, too, can deteriorate. Holiness, too, needs to be freshened, enlivened, disciplined—or else it will decay.

Finally, he ends chapter 1 with one of the clearest and most pungent sentences in the Rule: "Let us pass them by,"—hermits, sarabaites, and gyrovagues—he writes, "then with the help of God, proceed to draw up a plan for the strong kind, the cenobites."

And therein lies the spiritual point: Community itself is a spiritual act, a spiritual discipline, a spiritual force in society. No nonsense. No dishonesty. No posturing allowed. It is all a matter of being truly spiritual, truly dedicated to living a life of holiness, truly committed to a lifestyle that enriches life for us all. Just calling ourselves spiritual, religious, committed is not enough. It's a matter of what we really bring to the world, in and for the world community, that counts.

Benedict dismisses all but the cenobites, out of hand, those who live in community under a Rule and with a spiritual leader. The Rule of Benedict is clear: He is about creating a genuine spiritual community that can both proclaim the truth and nourish the world with its model.

Integrating the Practice

The answer to the question Why community? is deeply impacting. The truth is that only in community can you come to truly know yourself, as well as grow to the fullness of yourself. It's in community that your intentions, your goals, your gifts, your genuine spiritual depth—and your spiritual immaturity—are exposed and tested and stretched. Until you can finally become what you say you want to be—socially mature, psychologically developed, spiritually tried, tested, and sanctioned.

To have high ideals but a raging temper may well block the message of love that you say you value. To be generous with your ideas but selfish with your time may do a great deal to give a contrary message to God's love for immigrants. To work but fail to be a sign of the Gospel may well dampen the development of the spiritual life in others. The point is that you come to community to become the best of yourself, which means that the worst of yourself will surely be tempered there.

You come to community to find the core of life and share it with others. Community is the commitment to carry others through their periods of darkness as they carry you through yours.

It is about sustaining others and being sustained yourself when you have gone as far as you can go alone. The strength of community lies in the differences that diversity offers. The multiple gifts and cultures and insights of the various members provide the skills and resources, the vision and perseverance that great endeavors require. Community becomes the chain that binds the vision together.

It is exactly the community to which you belong—and the way you belong to it—that will determine what, in the end, becomes of your life. What the community as community believes and does and develops will mold what you really become.

A community's gift to the world is the sign that peace among strangers is possible. It is proof that the people who are not like you are exactly like you. Community reminds you that the human race cannot possibly thrive unless and until we open our arms to one another.

The nemeses of community are those who think that conformity in the name of unity is a substitute for the development of individual talents and ideas. Community is clear and living proof that it is precisely diversity that provides the resources needed to bring resilience, creativity, ingenuity, and vision to the task of humanizing humanity.

A community's common heart makes it a symbol of the humanization of humankind. As St. Basil wrote, Whose feet shall the hermit wash? Alone, your compassion is limited in scope and impact. But together, in community, you can create with others an arc of outreach wide enough to embrace the globe. Loving, openhearted human community can solve all the wars, begin all the peace, heal all the beaten women, release all the captive men, make sisters and brothers out of all the colors of all the immigrants of the globe. The Rule of Benedict gives the world a glimpse of what it takes to become loving communities and so to change the character of the world.

We come to community to find the core of life and share it with others. Community is the commitment to carry others through their periods of darkness as they carry us through ours. It is about sustaining others and being sustained ourselves when we have gone as far as we can go alone.

17

THE ORATORY

On Holy Space

An oratory is a small, private prayer space that enables moments of personal spiritual growth even in a frenetic, spiritually undersubscribed world.

We were driving in and out of the mountain passes, up and down the hills of Ireland, where the most common stopping places along the way were the "holy wells." These water spots, small shrines dedicated to the early saints of Ireland, mark the development of Celtic Christianity there. They brought alive for me a scene out of a church my generation had never known. I found myself putting two distant eras together, one out of the sixth-century Rule of Benedict, the other out of the institutional church that grew up across Europe centuries after that.

There is, in the middle of the Rule of Benedict, a simple, mundane sentence easily overlooked, seldom appreciated for the power of what it is saying: "Let the oratory be what it is called." *What?*

Years later, as I tried to figure out what the Rule really meant by such a sparse but simple sentence, I remembered the Skelligs, which I'd climbed when I was in Ireland. The Skelligs are two mountains that rise up in the Atlantic Ocean off the coast of

Kerry, where in the fourth century—the fourth century!—a monastic community at the top of one of the mountains lived in beehive huts around a small stone chapel. There, the tiny oratory as the center of the community was conspicuous and distinct.

The Church had not always been composed of grand sanctuaries and great cathedrals. If anything, in those early centuries, it had been a church of hidden spaces. The world knew more about catacombs than it did about Catholic churches. The architecture of the faith was growing, yes, but churches, as we know them in all their beauty, all their grandeur, were few and far between.

Churches came to be official worship spaces. Chapels, on the other hand, were small, simple, and unobtrusive memorials. Chapels, for a long time, had been marks of religion in every cult and culture everywhere; chapels were common. Benedict had clearly built one right in the middle of his monastery, and he wanted it, as in the monastic caves in the desert, to become the heart of the cenobitic community as well. He wanted it to become central to the consciousness of the monastics. "Let the oratory be what it is called"—not a conference room, not a schoolroom, not a parlor, not a waiting room, not extra cupboard space: an oratory.

Benedict wanted the architecture of the monastery itself to demonstrate that we all need to build into our lives a private space for God. Even in the middle of the bustle of our lives. He wanted this space to be off-limits to the world, a place of reflection.

Chapels grew up all over Europe. As holy wells grew up all over Ireland. They became local sanctuaries, decorated by local artists, where the pictures and rosaries and flowers hang to this day. They became a veritable geography of stopping points where people prayed, took their breath in the middle of a trek, and collected "holy water" to take back home to grace their own house shrines. These were places, small monuments, made for talking to God face-to-face.

But the really interesting thing about such hideaway prayer places is that small chapels are with us still. We build them into hospitals and airports, colleges and cemeteries. For everyone. Even when they're built under the auspices of a particular group, they often quickly become nondenominational, God-spaces, holy moments for everyone.

As the years went by, important families had private chapels on their own property, in their very houses, like in Indian homes where *puja,* the devotion at a shrine to a chosen god, took place. In those days, when churches were miles apart and cathedrals were overwhelmingly awesome, not made for small people and small events, it was the house and mountain chapels that invited prayer.

Now, in these times, we are at the very same kind of moment: Churches are closing as congregations move or disappear. Massive cathedrals stand alone in the cities, still cavernous, too often empty. Now, perhaps more than ever, we need to "let the oratory be what it is called." We must let it call us beyond our present overwhelmed selves. What will happen to our hearts if there is no place for us to find the beauty of emptiness in an overstuffed world? We live in an overnoisy, overcrowded, overstimulating round of events, with hardly a break to think through the important questions of life: What is life about? What is the purpose of our lives? How can we possibly make things better, more whole, for our families, for our world, for ourselves?

Integrating the Practice

Chapels are the call to "Come away and rest a while," as Mark, chapter 6, records Jesus' invitation to the disciples. But, as the

Rule of Benedict says, it's you who have to "let the oratory be what it is called." Which means that you have to make an oratory for yourself somehow: Take a long walk alone, perhaps, where the whipping wind or the bursting of the trees can bring you back to the essentials, the basics of life. The point is that your "oratory" is whatever invites you, lifts your soul beyond the daily and the mundane. The oratories of the heart are any place that recalls you to your spiritual self.

I have to build the arts back into my life, for instance, by standing in front of a small oil painting and asking myself what of the spirit it is saying to me. I must let it tell me what I am afraid to say myself—about how tangled my life is, about how alone I am, about how I have been ignoring the oratories of life. About the fact that I don't know how to pray or reflect at all anymore. Then I must turn those challenges of the psyche into a prayer.

How else shall I find peace if I do not seek it? There is no peace for the hardened heart, for the heart long years away from the spiritual part of the self. There is no joy for the dry heart. There is no freedom for the constricted heart. There is no life for the soul that lives only in the dank, dark thoughts of the present.

It may be the oratory you have not visited for years that waits to hear you empty your heart. Without rushing you, it slows you down long enough to hear your own needs. It calms you without demanding answers that take more time. It stretches you beyond irritations and deadlines to remember that the world of the soul is greater than the things that trap you in an arid dailiness.

The oratory tells you that you yourself must reach out, stop, sink down inside yourself, and let the weariness, the pain, the fear of abandonment evaporate and go to dust in the presence of the soothing warmth of faith and the promises of security, beauty, joy, and happiness that come with the presence of God in your life.

Benedict wanted the architecture of the monastery itself to demonstrate that we all need to build into our lives a private space for God. Even in the middle of the bustle of our lives. He wanted this space to be off-limits to the world, a place of reflection.

18

HERMITS

On the Solitary Life

Also called eremites are those persons who retire from society, primarily for religious reasons, and live in solitude. Christian hermits arose in the deserts of Egypt and Syria in the third century in response to the persecution of Christians and then the politicization of Christianity as the state religion of the Roman Empire.

I remember the situation as if it were yesterday. I was doing a speaking tour in Kenya, Tanzania, and Botswana, and spending time in monasteries of Benedictine women as I went. Most of all, I was learning more than I taught. In one instance, I learned more than I wanted to learn as well. The monastery I was staying in, they told me, had a hermit, a past Prioress, who when her term was over moved out of the main monastery to a small cabin hermitage and garden on the grounds. I became instantly alert. I was a past Prioress. I had given a great deal of thought to going to a hermitage as soon as my term would be over. It had been a long twenty years of administration. But I had no one with any kind of similar experience to talk to about it. This was my chance. By the time I worked up the nerve to ask for an appointment, she had already left word that she would like to meet me. Wonderful, I thought. Kindred souls. An act of God.

The tour of her hermitage took about five minutes. She lived in a big open room divided by a bedsheet. Behind the sheet was her prie-dieu and her altar. The space outside the prayer area had a small kitchen, a cot, and a reading area. Just enough, I thought. Now to talk for a while.

Our conversation, our dialogue, took little more time than the tour of this one-room hermitage had. "How does a person know that they're meant to be a hermit?" I asked.

"You?" she said. And I launched into the insistence of the thought, my love of quiet, the desire to be alone, the weight of all the travel, the deadlines, the struggle for the renewal of the Church and the liberation of women.

Without missing a breath, she looked me straight in the eye and said—plainly, crisply—"You are not a hermit." How can she say that with such certainty? She doesn't even know me, I said to myself.

Then, long pause and longer look. "You are not a hermit," she repeated. "If you went to a hermitage, you would be a hermit like Thomas Merton. You would have company every day."

I don't remember the goodbyes, but I have never forgotten the answer. She knew what I didn't. It's one thing to like quiet, silence, solitude. It's entirely another to choose those things for the right reason. Hermits go to hermitages to live their lives in God for the sake of the world. I wanted to go to a hermitage for my sake and leave the sake of the world behind.

End of conversation.

So here's what I learned as a result: In the ancient Church, hermits—the Greek word for "desert"—went to the desert to keep the spirit of the early Church vibrant and alive in a period of the secularization of the young Church. Christianity being acknowledged as the state religion of the Roman Empire did not make the entire population really Christian. That spirit could only be embodied by the most zealous of them—the Desert Monastics—who became the spiritual guides of those who sought their direction.

Hermits didn't just practice religion; they lived the spiritual life with all the asceticism that implied: fasting, praying, living simply, and, at the same time, making themselves available to the questions, the spiritual concerns, the needs of others. The difference is that they lived poverty, celibacy, and obedience separated or in clusters in the desert.

They became models of an alternative lifestyle. While the world went askew in cities designed for self-indulgence, monastics went on praying and counseling in the desert and supported themselves by making baskets to sell. Their example of asceticism, personal discipline, and spiritual fervor was set and, however small, is with us still.

Integrating the Practice

Hermits have arisen in every major tradition, including Jewish and Christian. Strains of Buddhism, Hinduism, Islam (Sufism), and Taoism also recognize hermits who commit themselves to an ascetic and solitary way of life as an important and legitimate dimension of their traditions.

To this day Christian hermits attach themselves to a diocese (Canon 603) and take their vows to the local bishop. Then they get small jobs to take care of themselves if necessary, and, like the judges of the Hebrew scriptures, sit at the edges of society, talking to those who seek insight into how to live a life not made of power, money, and prestige.

Anchorites—also hermits—have become wisdom figures.

While the rest of us perch on a high-wire act—trying to balance money with charity, peace with political power—they spend their lives in total dedication to the Word of God and become signs of its meaning for today. Hermits pursue life's great questions rather than its daily confusions. Unlike society around them, they have little interest in the new thing or the best thing or the biggest thing or the most expensive thing. They simply immerse themselves in the spiritual journey of life by passing on the flow of wisdom and insight as they go.

These monastics have withdrawn from the factions and biases around them in order to think more objectively than most of us have the luxury of doing. They make themselves available to those who, like me that day in Africa, have no one to talk to about their deepest concerns, their troublesome issues. The truth is that not only do we all seek the Way, but we all seek a companion, at various intervals, to walk it with us. And there, reading under the tree, if we're lucky, is the hermit in our midst who has nothing but time to listen to us struggle with the core of our lives.

Hermits seek God without the trappings of titles and résumés or badges of rank or achievement. They are countersigns of new perspectives under the principle that those who are most removed from any situation may be those who can see all sides of it clearly and stay closest to the essence of the problem.

Hermits' hospitality is spiritual hospitality. They receive people with an honesty that goes right to the heart of things. The spiritual heart of things—not the psychological heart of things or the commercial heart of things or the social heart of things. Hermits are not yesterday's Dear Abbys. They are today's oases of truth. Sources of Spirit left loose for all our sakes.

St. Benedict, remember, became a hermit himself after he left the spiritual debacle of Rome. Only when the shepherds begged him to leave the cave at Subiaco to teach others what he had taught them did he become the Benedict the spiritual world knows now.

May you who read this book take time in the private, internal deserts of your life to think, as Benedict and the hermits did, about what's going on in you and in the world now. May you take enough time for yourself to give thought to what you need to do to heal life as we know it as a result. Finally, may you live a holy life so that the world around you can never destroy the peace you have within.

Hermits didn't just practice religion; they lived the spiritual life with all the asceticism that implied: fasting, praying, living simply, and, at the same time, making themselves available to the questions, the spiritual concerns, the needs of others.

19

SOLITUDE

On Discovering Calm and Clarity

Monastics live a life of regular separation from others in order
to nourish the spiritual life and find the calm and clarity we
need to make our way through all the questions and crises
with which life confronts us.

The earliest thing I remember about my initiation into monastic life was not community meals or community chapter or assembly meetings or even community feast days and choir practice. What I remember most were the daily walks around and around the inner court of the monastery, alone and in silence. Perfect silence. The impact of it stays with me yet.

Solitude is a natural and regular part of the monastic life. It is the one place where we take the time and the space to go down into the depths, to confront ourselves about the way we're living it, to notice what's missing in it for us, to think through what we've been avoiding.

Solitude is a spiritual vacation for the soul. It gives us spiritual relief to finally be free to think deeply about the unending unanswerable questions that haunt us, both personal and spiritual, both private and global. Solitude is not a deprivation. Solitude is time set aside for us to discover the hidden kernels of the soul and give them light to grow in.

Who hasn't known the desire for solitude or the great burst of blessings that come with it? Not exactly immediately, perhaps, but someday, when the fog clears. The work of solitude has been seeded in our psyches to burst out just when we need it. Later.

The poet William Wordsworth put the whole essence of solitude in one poem when he wrote, "I wandered lonely as a cloud." It reads:

I wandered lonely as a cloud
That floats on high o'er vales and hills,
When all at once I saw a crowd,
A host, of golden daffodils;
Beside the lake, beneath the trees,
Fluttering and dancing in the breeze.

And, then, two stanzas later, he tells us what solitude has planted in him when he writes,

[And] oft, when on my couch I lie
In vacant or in pensive mood,
They flash upon that inward eye
Which is the bliss of solitude;
And then my heart with pleasure fills,
And dances with the daffodils.

The meaning is clear. Solitude is not an escape from life; it is the kind of immersion in quiet that enables us to look beyond the daily density of our lives. In solitude we begin to see things we hadn't really noticed before.

The monastic knows the truth of it: Life is actually a very rigidly organized enterprise that we fail to assess as often as it needs to be reviewed. The American merry-go-round takes over and life becomes a revolving door of doing without thinking and thinking without doing. Which is exactly when we need solitude enough to catch up, to think newly, to pray over, to concentrate on, to contemplate what it will take to do things differently. We need to put down the papers and the lists, the deadlines and the drone of it all.

Separation from others, solitude, gives us the distance, the concentration, and the insight we need to live well in a world teeming with talk, sound, noise, the pressures of the daily schedule, and the deadlines facing us tomorrow. Only solitude can provide the calm and quiet it takes to make the great decisions, to welcome the insights we need to achieve the happy, peaceful life we've been looking for.

Monasticism, on the other hand, has built solitude and peace right into its center. In fact, there are those who believe that without solitude, the healthy life is impossible.

Integrating the Practice

For years, researchers warned the world of the dangers of solitude to mental health. And if you are talking about imprisonment, mental anguish and withdrawal, rejection and social isolation, it's true. Involuntary solitude has even been classified as torture. But with solitude that is sought after, used wisely, and becomes a part of life, the world knows now what monasticism has known for thousands of years: Solitude rinses the soul of noise and clutter, frees the heart to sing, and gives life another whole level of worth.

It's when you, like Jesus, as scripture puts it, "go apart for a while" that you get to know yourself. You find out, if you'll listen, exactly what it is that is driving you. You also find out what it is that is weighing you down—even in the best of lives.

Space and time spent in solitude are a kind of independence training. They free you from the pressures and expectations of the people around you. You learn to take responsibility for yourself—outside the realm of those who want to direct you to their choices, lead you to their opinions, shape you into copies of themselves. But only in solitude can you really hear yourself think the big thoughts that plot your way ahead in life.

Soon, solitude begins to be a refuge for you. Being on the porch alone, walking around the pond, fishing on the public dock—all spaces that are more than space but rather the beginnings of the maturity of the self. Clarity of thought comes, and with it a new kind of self-esteem when I'm not comparing myself to others.

The point, every monastic knows—as do community people all—is that to grow up you have to separate from the group or you will forever define yourself by the group and be determined only by its values and goals of the group. Solitude saves you from that by growing you to the point where you really know who you are, what your aspirations are, what your choices are. Through the practice of solitude, you come to know—eventually undoubtedly—that you can survive without the group; you can define yourself; you can be all right alone; you can become what you want to be whether anybody else sees that path for you or not.

It is a great moment in life, this freeing of the self. But all of it must be dug out of the cement of your own soul. Once you take the risk of being alone with it, in the presence of God with it—your life wakes up inside yourself.

As Wordsworth said,

[And] oft, when on my couch I lie
In vacant or in pensive mood,
They flash upon that inward eye
Which is the bliss of solitude;
And then my heart with pleasure fills,
And dances with the daffodils.

You know now the power of solitude to sustain you and, most of all, to confirm that the spiritual embryo in you has become a new kind of spiritual stolidity.

Solitude is a spiritual vacation for the soul. It gives us spiritual relief to finally be free to think deeply about the unending unanswerable questions that haunt us by the day, both personal and spiritual, both private and global.

20

BLESSING

On Recognizing the Gifts of Life

The rite of blessing is a formal ritual intended to dedicate a person or thing to the service of God—as in the blessing of an infant in the sacrament of baptism or an adult in ordination or the marriage rite. Blessings also invoke the favor of God in the doing of the service itself—as in the invocation of safety for departing medical personnel into a toxic area.

In our monastery we bless everything: the house on New Year's Day, the work commitments of each of the sisters, each other as the community processes into chapel. Blessing is the invisible chain in community life.

The word *blessing* itself comes from the Hebrew scriptures and means a favor from God. To seek or offer blessings is certainly one of the most ancient of monastic traditions, but it is also a human act that crosses all races, cultures, denominations, and religious families. Blessing, it seems, is the cry of the human heart for ongoing divine protection and support. The question is always, Why would such a thing be so universal? But the answer is just as clear and constant.

Blessings—the good things, the challenges, even the difficulties of life—lead us back to a provident God, the Source of Life and all its gifts. We bless God—or praise this Source of Life for the joys and gifts of life. We bless others—we wish them the on-going awareness of such favors. We bless the events and emotions that seem at first to endanger our lives and our happiness—like death, or job loss, or distress—knowing that, in the end, good will come from the God who created us, loves us, and maintains us through all the exigencies of life.

We bless, as well, the objects we dedicate to the service and praise of God: our monasteries, our churches, our lands, our altars and temples and shrines and memorials, which are silent remind-ers of the presence of God from one end of the world to the other. We surround ourselves in praise of God, in awareness of the gifts of God. As a result, blessings create a kind of bridge between heaven and earth. There is, in fact, no time in life that is not marked with a blessing.

In every human heart, from people in every lifestyle and tradi-tion, there is an awareness of a kind of Divine Goodness that en-velops us all. It is in that ambience that we seek to live. Babies are blessed, marriages are blessed, ordinations are blessed, dedications are blessed, consecrations are blessed. Or to put it another way, love, care, health, birth, death—every turning point of life is blessed. Which means that the universe is full of goodwill, of great respect, of care, and of love, if not understanding, of the Creative Force that brings us forth. There is an invisible consciousness that everything we need to sustain us on the path is with us already. That's what we praise and pray for.

The practice of blessing, in fact, crosses all denominational boundaries in recognition of the one God who sustains us all. Blessings are then the very ground of universal peace. Of human unity and common-heartedness across the various racial cultures. Of hope in a common future together.

From the time of the Desert Monastics to this world of quantum physics and nuclear power, monastics pronounce life a "blessing" from God. We pronounce, that is, that we are not our own keepers. We are not the sources of our own lives. We live in the womb of God and delight in this unknowing, this glory of life, this blessing of all times and all peoples. And we pronounce it alive in our tiny little lives, as well, in the hope that we do not take the good things of life, in all their glory, for granted.

Integrating the Practice

The Rule of Benedict records specific times that the community is to ask God to give a member special help in carrying out community duties. These passages have to do with the effect of the member's service on the rest of the community. All these blessings teach us something about our own very routine, very polite, but, too often, unconscious social lives.

First, the Abbot or Abbess/Prioress is required to bless the community at the end of each segment of prayers during the Liturgy of the Hours. With prayer finished, the members are to return to the duties of the day. The implication is clear: Fervor during prayer is not enough to make a good monastic. We are each to serve the physical needs of the community, just as any family expects the fullness of responsibility from one another, and the Abbot/Abbess/Prioress blesses those whose works will care for the rest of us.

Second, Table Readers begin their week of public reading during monastic mealtimes—a teaching moment for what then would have been largely illiterate communities, many of whom could not read. Then the leader of the community asks for divine grace for the reader who will perform what is actually a highly educational task, so that the entire community may learn from it.

That point is clear, too: Only those able to read should be allowed to read, Benedict instructs us. It is interesting that this is the one time when Benedict requires a particular talent for serving the community. He writes in chapter 38 of the Rule, "Members will read and sing, not according to rank, but according to their ability to benefit their hearers." Willingness is no substitute for preparation, for ability, for serious commitment to a task that will benefit—or not—every member of the community.

Third, the kitchen servers of the week, who prepare and serve the food, are given a formal blessing by the Abbess before they begin their service. Like the requirement to read well so that the community can be nourished intellectually, this blessing begs that for the sake of the community, these cooks will nourish the community well physically. After all, the produce of the land God made provides what the community needs most at the time: energy and good health. Good food, well prepared, provides life for one another, for the poor of the area, and for the hungry travelers who stop by on the way to somewhere else.

And finally, in one other place, the Rule of Benedict prescribes a blessing: Older monastics bless younger monastics who pass them throughout the day. By this one small act, the young of the community are connected to the wisdom of the elders so that the pillars of the tradition may never be dismissed by the generations to come. These blessings are simple gestures that recognize the gifts of those who have carved the tradition before us: "Bless God," says the younger; "Bless you, dear child," says the elder; or we say in the same mind to our benefactors, "May God bless your generosity as you are blessing to others."

Little gestures, indeed. But in the end, they become resounding moments of recognition, of awareness that we are not worlds unto ourselves. That we are created and sustained not by our own hands, but by the Creator and by the service and care of those around us.

Indeed, your blessings are small gestures, but—perhaps, maybe, someday—they will save the world from itself and touch your own heart with consciousness of the fundamental grace and blessing of life, however limited, however enjoyed, despite the particulars of wealth, responsibility, and moral purpose.

There is an invisible consciousness that everything we need to sustain us on the path is with us already. That's what we praise and pray for.

21

DIVINE OFFICE

On the Daily Presence of God

The praying of the official prayer of the Church by clergy, religious, or laity, called the Divine Office, is based entirely in scripture. Jewish psalms, hymns, and readings from the Hebrew and Christian scriptures are its basis and make it a lifelong spiritual guide.

The Liturgical Hours, collectively called the Divine Office, have a long, long history reaching back into Judaism, through the life of Jesus. And yet, they have an equally immediate value for us, today, here, in this world. Which, of course, is why they never go away.

The psalms recited during the Liturgical Hours grow out of Jewish tradition and history. After the destruction of the Temple, the Jewish community began to pray at regular hours to mark their continuing fidelity. Instead of animal sacrifices for the forgiveness of sin, now that the altar and the Holy of Holies had been destroyed, they concentrated on practicing "a sacrifice of praise" instead.

As Christianity evolved and took its place in the new world of Israel, Greece, Rome, the Mediterranean, and the Byzantine Empire, the new faith organized itself into a creed, a theology, a way of worship. The Divine Office, following the civic hours of Rome, became the Liturgical Hours of the monastic day. The "hours" or periods of prayer took form. Matins, the early morning prayer; Lauds at dawn; Prime, Terce, Sext, and None, once the hours of the changing of the guard at the shrine of the Roman god Jupiter at what would now be the third, sixth, ninth, and noon hours of the day, and, finally, Vespers at dusk and Compline at night, led the Christian community through the memory of God as the day passed.

These prayers became the heartbeat of the pious life. More than that, however, this round of Divine Hours became the community's daily immersion in scripture: in the Gospels, the Letters of Paul, the feast days, and, of course, the psalms and prayers ascribed to each of them.

The 150 psalms that emerged over the centuries trace the faith, the pain, the struggles, the gratitude, and the hope in God, who had first delivered the Hebrews from Egypt and who, they knew, would deliver them again from the pitfalls, the snares, and the dark places of life. Those prayers—the psalms that trace the arc of God's presence with us—form the basis of what are yet today the Liturgical Hours for Christians.

Over time, these psalms, meant to go on connecting the hearts of the seekers with the heart of God, became the pillar of prayer in them. The psalms recalled for them the memory of God's power, their trust in God's faithfulness, the breadth of what it means "to search for God in life." The heartbeat of the Spirit in them took the faithful from beginning to end of every day until we, like those before us, flourish in this revelation of God's ongoing liberation, of God's ongoing counsel, in life, even this life, our life.

Just as important as their personal power in our private lives, however, is the awareness that in the psalms, Judaism, Christianity, and Islam share a common path to God. Human community becomes a cosmic reality. Islamic scholars are convinced that David, to whom so many of the psalms are attributed, as a singer, poet, and prophet, is a bridge for religious understanding among the three religions.

It is that great spiritual connectivity which the psalms, generations later, fan into flame in the Abrahamic family. In a world of tautening geopolitical conflict, that common prayer bond is no small gift. Daily, those three religions remember that we are each a common strand of worship originally planted by Abraham. To the Jews, Abraham is the base and center of Judaism. To the Christians, it is out of Abraham's call that once Christian Jews eventually became Christian. And to Muslims, it is through Hagar, Abraham's concubine and mother of Abraham's son Ishmael, that what we know as Islam eventually came.

Ironically, it is prayer that keeps us all one step further away from the kind of denominationalism that makes us enemies rather than companions on the Way.

As constant as the psalms have been over the years, however, it was St. Benedict in the sixth century who arranged and ordered them for Christian usage across all levels of society. In the mind of Benedict, fidelity to the Liturgical Hours was the ground of spiritual development. Monastic prayer revolves around the psalms and raises one generation after another to understand the ways of God as we grow, both alone and together.

Having arranged the psalms for daily prayer, Benedict leaves us with more than an order of use. Instead, monastic prayer—the psalms themselves—became an entrée to all the challenges of life, not an escape from them. Applied to our own world here and now, the psalms immerse us in the consciousness of God alive in our lives. That monastic insight would be shared with the rest of the Western world for centuries in prayer, in lectio, in community, in work.

Clearly, the Divine Office is not a regime, a schedule, a structure on which to hang our prayer life. Rather, it is an immersion in the ways of God with humanity and ways of life on the way to God. It is the Divine Office, the Liturgical Hours, that steep us in the Word of God all our lives, reminding us daily of the pain, the sorrow, the support and praise of God that grows the thinking Christian from mere recitation of prayers to the kind of adult prayerfulness that embraces the needs of the entire world.

Integrating the Practice

Prayer in the Benedictine mind is all about going deeper and deeper into the Mystery of the Christian life with God. It calls you to reach out every day of your life for the presence of God and prepares you, perhaps unconsciously, without your even knowing it, for all the demanding life moments yet to come. The Divine Office is a symbol of the Christian community in prayer for the entire world and especially for the poorest of the poor. It stretches you beyond your singular self to provide for and protect the little ones of the world. God, the psalmist says, who has always sent salvation to the needy, now sends you to them as well.

Most of all, the psalms call all of us to see ourselves as part of the larger human community, to be conscious of the pain of the world, of our own obligations to respond to it, and, always, of the eternal presence of God whatever the circumstances with which we grapple.

This prayer is communal; it is also personal; it remains forever sharply committed to the human condition. No flowery escapism here, no notion whatsoever that God is distant and disinterested in your existence. The Liturgical Hours call you to sing the psalms of sadness, of joy, of praise, of trust, of faith, and of fear and anger and lament, all the human emotions—the whole gamut of what it means to be human—and then to deal with them in your own most humane way.

The Divine Office—this work of God in you—is the lifeline of your life. Through it you pray for yourself; you pray for those who cannot pray for themselves. You pray for the world, for the Church, for the people of God; and, like the psalmist before you, you pray to be strong enough to find God in darkness as well as in light. Always.

Within the last five thousand years some unknown psalmist wrote, "You have not handed me over to my enemy, but set my feet free . . ." (Ps. 31:8). And we are still singing verses like that today. Why? Because it is a human emotion—this sense of liberation. Because it reminds us all of the effects of an experience—of being freed from oppression or social danger—that is still valid, still crying for expression somewhere now. It is, for instance, still in the hearts of those who survived the Holocaust, of those who went through the coronavirus pandemic, maybe. Or the awfulness of unbearable debt. Or the shame and danger of social rejection, perhaps. Or, worse, because it is still on the lips of the one who moved just as the drone dropped its bomb next to him.

Nothing has changed. Humanity is humanity—with all its pain and all its arrogance. All its neediness and all its pomp. It is these things that psalmic prayer is about.

In monastic life, every prayer is a recognition of what life is like with God—and without God. It's about remembering and praying for the people outside your window who are still struggling to escape "the counsel of the wicked" or are sick with the knowledge that they are captive to something. The beauty is that developing the senses of the soul is really what going to prayer is about. It is about watching yourself grow up—spiritually.

As the bells ring the various times of daily prayer in a monastery, we turn again and again to the consciousness of God in our lives. Marked off by the Liturgical Hours, which are steeped in the struggles of the soul, the searching of the mind, and the pleadings of the heart, monastics preserve a sense of the continuing presence of God, hour by hour by hour, in our lives.

Most of all, the psalms call all of us to see ourselves as part of the larger human community, to be conscious of the pain of the world, of our own obligations to respond to it, and, always, of the eternal presence of God whatever the circumstances of life with which we each grapple.

22

MANUAL LABOR

On the Purpose of Work

In distinguishing between cenobites—communal
monastics—and other types of religious common to the era,
the Rule of Benedict cites work as the fundamental
difference. Benedict says of cenobites: "When they live by the
labor of their hands as our ancestors and the apostles did,
then they are really monastics."

Ora et labora—prayer and work—is one of the oldest tags applied to Benedictine monasteries. Though it is not the official motto of the Benedictine Order, it is, nevertheless, the best known. It is a window into the values we hold dear, but it also provides a kind of universal understanding of the relationship between those two poles.

There are multiple stories in the folklore of monasticism that give us a feeling for the valuation of work in the monastic life. "Teacher," the disciples said, "how can our work approach the works of our ancestors?" And the elder answered: "Just as our ancestors Abraham, Isaac, and Jacob all invented new ways of serving—so we are all meant to devise some kind of work for ourselves and thus be of service to others."

Benedict was quite clear about the place of work as an important piece of monastic spirituality. He talks about work in two major chapters of the Rule and then identifies special community responsibilities in a number of others. In chapter 48, "Daily Manual Labor," and in chapter 35, "Kitchen Servers of the Week," of the Rule, he lays out the attitudes the monastic must bring to work. There is no doubt that he places work on the same level he places prayer as a necessary dimension of monastic life.

The sacred work of the monastic is the Divine Office or Opus Dei—the work of God and lectio. This work of God, the praise and practice of the will of God, is the monastic's lifetime concentration. But then there is the manual work of taking in the harvest that will sustain both the community and the surrounding area. And just as important, there are the works of service needed to maintain the physical and familial needs of the community itself. Finally, Benedict cites the intellectual work and study required to deepen the monastic's spiritual life and human understanding as the years go by.

Work, in other words, enriches and develops life on all levels. Its quality rests on two principles:

First, Benedict teaches that "idleness is the enemy of the soul" and that we are all important. Work is the discipline that keeps us involved in every dimension of the communal life. Every monastic in the monastery—young and old—is to be given a task to help maintain it, one way or another.

Second, that work is a commitment to God's service. Therefore, monks are to have specified periods of both manual labor and study. No one just drops in and "helps around." We all carry the monastery together, both its physical and its intellectual works or ministries.

Subsistence, asceticism, internal and external service, and almsgiving for the needs of the poor direct the lives of monastics beyond themselves. The spiritual life does not give us the right to be waited on by everybody else because our work is higher. On the contrary. It is our spiritual and intellectual lives which demand that we give ourselves away.

In today's world, the effect of whatever work each of us does—intellectual, artistic, social, communal, or individual—must be good for the globe as well as for the local area and the particular monastery.

Integrating the Practice

"Work," the poet Kahlil Gibran writes, "is love made visible." And the Book of Ecclesiastes puts it squarely. "There is a time to gain," it says. There is a time, in other words, to develop the best in yourself so that you can make a difference for everyone else.

The most telling indicator of the spiritual deterioration of the Western world may well be its distortion of the purpose of work. In this culture we work so that we can do something other than work as soon as possible. We work for personal profit, not for the good of the human race. And we routinely work at segmented tasks that have no overarching meaning to us. But motives like those flirt with moral schizophrenia. Without a sense of purpose in life and a sense of obligation to leave the world better than we found it, we can work in places that dump chemicals into lakes and rivers without a quiver of conscience.

We can spend our lives dallying in false advertising and slick brochures about the sale of barren land and cheap trinkets, and never for a moment wince at the dishonesty of it. We can turn mornings into one long coffee break, and accept a wage for doing it, and never even have the grace to blush. Then we wander listless for years, wondering what our lives are really all about. "We build statues out of snow," the poet Walter Scott says, "and weep to see them melt."

Yet the basic questions of life are What am I doing? and Why am I doing it? Who profits from what I do and who does not? To spend my life answering those questions alone could change the world for millions. Indeed, what the world needs is a spirituality of work. But major obstacles to a spirituality of cocreation run deep in our society. The strains of self-gratification underlie both our motives and our interests. What we do and why we do it begin and end with ourselves to the point that social crises—homelessness, malnutrition, lack of medical care, and poverty—have become marks of the character of our society rather than targets for our compassion and conditions our country works to ameliorate.

We are taught at a very early age to work for ourselves alone: our money, our status, our security are what counts, not the quality of our society as a whole. The notion that individuals can have whatever individuals can get turns greed into virtue. We criticize welfare for the poor, which we call food stamps, but have no problem at all with welfare for the rich, which we call tax breaks. We use the poor of other countries to provide labor at slave wages. We export our jobs but not our wage scales. We use work to exploit people rather than to liberate them. We pay Indian children pennies per hour to work seventy-hour weeks making our shoes and deprive our own working poor of just wages and benefits. Indeed, we need new ideals of work.

A spirituality of work, the ancient Rule of Benedict implies, has five components. It sees work as your gift to the world. It builds the human community. It leads to self-fulfillment. It saves you from total self-centeredness and gives you a reason to exist that is larger than yourself. And it enables the Creator to go on creating. Clearly, work sanctifies you by calling you to save the globe for others and save others for the sake of the globe.

Once upon a time, past the seeker on a prayer rug came the

beggars and the broken and the beaten. Looking up to heaven, the seeker cried out, "Great and loving God, if you are a loving God, look at these and do something!" And the voice came back from heaven, "I did do something—I made you."

A spirituality of work is that process by which you finally come to know that your work is God's work, unfinished by God because God meant it to be finished by you.

The basic questions of life are What am I doing and why am I doing it? Who profits from what I do and who does not? To spend my life answering those questions alone could change the world for millions.

23

SERENITY

On Inner Peace

Peace is the official motto of the Benedictine Order and all of
its monasteries. It is both a description of Benedictine life
and a welcome to those who come to the community for
prayer, quiet, rest, and personal support.

Over the archways of medieval Benedictine monasteries shone
one phrase: *Pax intrantibus*—Peace to those who enter here.
Nothing could be more basic, nothing more soulful where monasticism is concerned. But this motto has a far more complex
meaning than most people surmise. Yes, it means that monasteries
are quiet and peaceful places. But, at the same time, monastic
peace is a much deeper concept.

As Europe's Pax Romana began to deteriorate, it was monasticism that restored order in communities that gathered around the
monasteries. People flocked to them, looking for peace. It was for
the sake of Benedictine peace, after all, that, as the Rule said, "all
guests . . . are to be welcomed as Christ." Monastics had no enemies, refused to make enemies, and did nothing by force. Monasteries were places where anyone could come and there would be
somebody to welcome them, to take them in, to accept who and
what they were.

In the face of social chaos, the monasteries brought back social order, provided sustenance, and were based on spiritual values. People settled down in the shadow of the monastery, where work could be had with regularity, where life went on with a sense of sufficiency, where slavery did not exist, where peace reigned. Monasticism provided a whole new way of being alive. It created communities of common ownership and shared wealth, the kinds of communities no one dreamed possible then and few dream possible now. Except that for over fifteen hundred years they've been the ground of vowed religious life—and they've worked.

Monastic communities were led by authority figures who emerged from the communities themselves. They were chosen from the community, by the community. They were not determined by either crown or sword. It was not on the basis of power and force that they ruled. On the contrary. Monastic obedience was based on listening to the needs of the members.

Benedictine communities did not function by punishment, or by control. The needs of human growth and spiritual development were what dictated the turns and twists of the community. And so those communities burgeoned and those monastics lived in quiet and peace when everything around them was in flames from the continued wars for power and control that drove medieval society.

The monasteries' witness of peace toward one another—strangers from strange places—created a new social system in the midst of the old. The Rule simply outlawed hostility and destruction of the peace among the members themselves: "No one has the authority to . . . strike any member of the community," it reads. End of discussion in a war-torn world. It is out of this worldview that this frail little Rule has preserved monastic peace for over fifteen hundred years. It is out of this worldview that monasticism modeled the kind of peace that was internal as well as external, personal as well as public.

Wanderers displaced by war and famine came to the kind of monastic stability that Benedictine communities promised. They came to islands of tranquillity, signs to everyone that peace was possible if we could only tame the tempers within us and live for the welfare of all rather than the gain of a few. Underlying it all, *pax*—peace—describes not only the nature of Benedictine life but the very gift of monasticism.

Monasticism is the call to develop to the best of ourselves, to the whole of ourselves. It leads us to the kind of faith in God which trusts that doing the will of God will bring us all to fullness of life. It calls us to put down our petty agitations, our nervous little worries. It invites us to go with the flow, to renounce our need to control our world. It calls us to bring heart to life as well as efficiency and order. It believes that God will see us through.

Peace—personal faith and trust in the heart of God—is actually what, at base, it's all about. Then as now, now as then, behind all the daily schedules and seasonal harvests, liturgical hospitality and ministry to many, one clearly important facet goes quietly on: the need to be peaceful ourselves if we are ever to bring peace to others.

Integrating the Practice

Personal transformation was the very goal of the vowed life. Interior quiet—the ability to be stretched beyond ourselves by living a life in search of God—is at the core of monasticism. Quietly, faithfully, lovingly—peacefully—a little at a time, we learn that life is lived in seasons, perhaps, or that patience is the ground of maturity, maybe, or that serious reflection is a richer way to live than as impulsive adolescents all our lives.

In a monastic world, decisions depend on prayerful discernment, not on personal emotional demands that come and go with the winds of change. Instead, equality and community—respect and common care—are the portals of a peaceful world, the presence in flesh and blood of a world that is capable of living in harmony, each of us the support of the other.

Personal peace is cultivated by practice and practiced by living a life of quiet openness to life itself, of trusting receptivity that does not collapse in the face of crisis. There are specific dimensions of peace, of course, each of which gets more and more engrained in the soul by the season:

First, monasticism deliberately cultivates quiet in us. It takes a long view of life. The good that does not exist yet is coming, is even now on the way, the monastic believes. Provided we prepare our hearts to receive it.

Second, genuine reflection on major issues, the core of monasticism, takes deep thought and serious analysis. It is wisdom that refuses to react to an idea before it reflects on it. Personal control may not be possible in a maelstrom of change that upends the world. When the answer is not clear, the monastic heart, steeped in quiet and faith, waits for it.

Third, in monastic life, interiority sustains us. It shields us from giving ourselves over to reactions without reason.

Finally, contemplation, the transcendence of the earthly to the comprehension of the spirit of life, is simply too profound to be diluted by concentrating on the ephemeral, the immediate, the superficial, the fleeting.

Which means what? It means that to have peace, to be really monastic, to be a monastic peacemaker, you can't fake it; you have to be it. In the family, in the city, at work, wherever your world hopes for peace, for the proof of peace, and the hope of peace, you must become it yourself. Rather than hope for it, bewail its ab-

sence, or chastise the world for lacking it, you must both bring it
and be it. The model of Benedict's monasteries lives on as a har-
binger of a peace that is both internal and external, both personal
and public. Wherever monasteries are to this day, this is the kind
of boundless peace that characterizes the authenticity of their centeredness.

Are you and I part of that quiet and quieting spirit yet? Both
by learning to control our own excesses and by helping to bring
calm and peace to the lives of others, monastic peace provides a
center to every storm in life. It is that for which the world waits in
each of us.

As a result, the relationship between public and personal peace
is integral to both global development and personal wholeness.
It's that universal call to public peace as well as to personal calm
that marks the monastic presence everywhere. Clearly Benedictine peace achieves the personal tranquillity that silence and contemplative calm bring to a person. But in the end, it makes for an
even farther-reaching contrast to the drumming, stomping, noise-
making emptiness of a digital world that fills the spectrum of
sound waves around it.

**Then as now, now as then, behind all the daily schedules and
seasonal harvests, liturgical hospitality and ministry to many,
one clearly important facet goes quietly on: the need to be
peaceful ourselves if we are ever to bring peace to others.**

24

LAUDS

On Morning Praise

**Lauds, chanted at daybreak, is a prayer of praise reserved
for the first liturgical hour of the day.**

Lauds happens when we wake up, which is one of the most
interesting things about it. The fact is that we get up to face a
day undone, uncompleted, not even started. And yet, before we
have a thing to be thankful for and facing a lot of things we don't
want to do, Benedict has us begin with praising God for the day
that is yet to come.

Listen carefully, Psalm 66 is clear: Praise is a necessary dimension of life. Not a nice dimension of life. A necessary dimension
of life. And so the psalm Benedict uses to open the Office of Lauds
is an unrelenting paean of praise and gratitude: It requires the
community to pray aloud:

> Shout joyfully to God, all you on earth;
> and proclaim God's name.
> Render glorious praise;
> say to the God of all life,
> "How tremendous your deeds!

Because of the greatness of your strength
your enemies yield to you.
Before you all the earth shall bow,
shall sing to you
sing to your name!"

And so the question, Why this psalm instead of one of the other possible 149 psalms in this ancient Book of the Hebrew scriptures that could have been chosen to start a monastic's day? The choice has to give us pause. After all, the Divine Office is not a collection of randomly selected prayers. There's a message here.

The fact is that the Office of Lauds actually requires us to re-think life and our attitudes toward it before we even think of be-ginning another day. Better yet, for the first time—in this world of ours—it is science that gives us an insight into the kind of spirituality Benedict wanted to build into our lives by opening the day with this particular psalm.

Indeed, we are at a strange and wonderful place in the process of human development and understanding. Science is helping us to see a little more about what it means to be human. As a result, harsh penances, the neurotic search for "perfection," the very no-tion that anyone can go through life without failure, without strain, without the slow, slow recognition of our own limitations makes life more livable, makes spirituality a positive practice. So we have, for the most part, stopped separating the spiritual ele-ments of our lives from the material dimensions as if they were two completely different aspects of us. As if we were each two different people, one part made for heaven, the other part earthy, inferior, made, at best, for taming the human in us. As a result of that kind of thinking, we too often miss the fact that what affects our physical lives affects our spiritual selves as well. One aspect of our humanity affects the other. One feeds the other. One dimension of us makes the other dimension real.

Until we begin to see our humanity as the bridge between the spiritual and the material, we're likely to spend a great deal of time praying simply because we're supposed to pray, or meditating because it makes us seem spiritual. When the truth is that to be whole we have to face the fact that one aspect of life is the gateway to the other. The spirit inspires us to grow to the fullness of ourselves; the body enables us to experience the growth of that spirit seriously, consciously, emotionally. And, lo, when we're full of praise—we come to realize—we also become full of joy.

That's why the liturgical hour of Lauds is so important. Lauds is the hinge of this union of spirit and body. Lauds, the song sung in praise of God, is, as well, the song sung in gratitude for all the good things in life. It is those good things, we come to realize, that are themselves signs, marks, proofs of the goodness of God, the goodness of life, and, most of all, on the sharp edge of the morning, the goodness of the daily.

Benedict begins our daily consciousness of God in the awareness that the goodness of God is among us, in us, around us at all times. And most of all, that we should begin nothing without being conscious of that. Whatever happens this day, the psalm prods us to remember, is a gift. Lauds is the consciousness that moves us to gratitude and so, eventually, to a steady, heart-beating happiness always.

Integrating the Practice

Lauds is one of the three major prayer periods in the Divine Office of the Western Christian Church. It is also, we know, traditionally said or chanted at daybreak. Think carefully. Why would

Lauds be the first prayer of the day? Why would early morning be the best time to say it?

At first glance, Lauds appears, at best, to be a peculiar use of the conundrum of time. What can we possibly be praising God for at the first moment of a day that has not even really started yet? And why?

Are we thanking God that we are alive? Well, maybe, but it's hard to say what that will do to freshen the soul of a person weighed down by what they know will be the burdens of the day. Or, if I'm not a morning person and can barely concentrate on anything at that hour, what good is "morning prayer"? Or are we praising God for the fact that we have managed to work up to any interest in life at all? At least at this hour of the day? Or is this one of those pieties meant to convince us that singing eternal alleluias in heaven is what the spiritual life is really all about?

It's questions like these that point us not at pious fervor, as important as we once thought that kind of prayer might be, but directly at science. Science knows now why being grateful is the very best thing we can do for ourselves to get life straight and happy and meaningful. Why pray Lauds first thing in the day? Because Lauds is about praise—about gratitude—and gratitude, we know now, is about enhancing our happiness.

The research is clear: Those who consciously express gratitude for at least three to five components of their lives every week are simply happier than those who don't. Research in the field of Martin E. P. Seligman's Positive Psychology affirms these findings over and over again. When we are consciously grateful for life, when we praise all the goodness in our lives, we make our lives happier. According to Positive Psychology, there are five areas of our lives that are directly affected by the degree of gratitude we bring to them: our emotional well-being, our social life, our personality, our career benefits, and our physical health.

Praise and gratitude for the good things in life—expressed consciously and regularly—change the way you react, the way you interact with other people, the way you progress in life, the way you feel about yourself. Your expressions of gratitude for the gifts of life determine the attitude and energy you bring with you into every challenge and relationship in life. Lauds is the celebration of all of them.

The question is simply, How are you cultivating the gratitude it takes for you to be content, to discover that happiness is the gift, not the need to have more and more? Life's slow and winding ways give you enough time to really appreciate what, frankly, still feels pretty humdrum. People whose lives are not lived on the mountain peaks of the world commonly forget that the shallows have a beauty of their own.

The quality of life you make for yourself depends on the way you approach praise and gratitude. Life, after all, really is what you do with it. Life is not what God does with it on your behalf. On the contrary. Defining God as the stage manager of life is one of the great mistakes of life. Worse, it is a seriously incorrect definition of God. Realizing that God the Creator trusts you to turn life into the happiness God means it to be is the essence of the truly spiritual life.

At Lauds, morning after morning, the monastic concentrates on the good things of life that God has created for us and so gets happier and happier as the years go by.

Benedict begins our daily consciousness of God in the awareness that the goodness of God is among us, in us, around us at all times. Whatever happens this day, the psalm prods us to remember, is a gift. Lauds is the consciousness that moves us to gratitude and so, eventually, to a steady, heart-beating happiness always.

25

VESPERS

On Evening Praise

**Vespers—Evensong—is the second of the three major hours
of the Divine Office and the last prayer of the monastic day.
It is also the most publicly beloved of the hours and
is often still celebrated in many countries.**

Psalm 9, the first of the psalms allocated to Vespers by the Rule
of Benedict, prays:

> I will praise you, O God, with all my heart;
> I will recount all your wonders
> and sing the glory of your name.
>
> My enemies turn back;
> as you confront them
> they stumble and perish.

Vespers, like Lauds, brings the monastic to a new kind of consciousness of life. Lauds calls for praise and gratitude at the beginning of the day. Vespers is said at dusk. At this hour, Benedict calls
us to end the day in a spirit of thanksgiving. Vespers celebrates
another day of God's presence in our lives. It calls us to go into the

night thankful for having survived the challenges of the day. It leaves us full of trust that the darkness shall not overcome us.

Religious life, in most of its forms, has two major characteristics. The first is its commitment to personal spiritual growth; the second is its dedication to caring for the world. The fact is that religious communities everywhere have worked hard to make the world a better place, and thanked God that they were also able to support masses of people who have been left out of the economic, educational, and societal mainstream.

In Lent, for instance, Benedict says we should deprive ourselves of a little meat and eat a little less than usual. But most of all, he wanted monastics to do a little more reading. He wanted us to do something that would stretch our minds and our souls and our all-round spiritual growth. "We are about to establish a school of the Lord's service," the Rule says in the Prologue, "in which we hope to introduce nothing harsh or burdensome." It's over fifteen centuries later, and that Rule is still defined as moderate, balanced, supportive.

At the same time, public mythology to the contrary, one element of religious life has been largely misunderstood. Religious communities have never been designed to deliberately threaten the health, life, or mental balance of their members in the name of holiness. Of course, some individuals, I'm sure, fasted too much, slept too little, were excessive in devising "penances" to purify their very natural impulses, like anger or envy or jealousy or acedia—apathy and diffidence, laziness and disinterest in doing anything of value. But penances or excessive discipline were not at the base of religious life. Not Benedictine life, certainly, which set out to live the ordinary life extraordinarily well. And so, true to that instinct, Vespers calls all of us to rest—not to spiritual extremes or physical deprivations.

Immediately after Vespers, at about 6:00 P.M., monastics went to bed. Supper was over, night was already here, the sky was dimming if not already dark. In a culture without lightbulbs, that means that monastics slept at least seven hours—7:30 P.M. to between 2:00 and 3:00 A.M.—before they "rose for the night hours," Matins and Lauds. They were clearly not being deprived of sleep. They prayed the long hours of the Office during the night and, after breakfast, worked in the monastery workshops and fields during the day. In our own culture, which routinely stays up until after the eleven o'clock news and then has to be up, out of the house, and in the office by at least eight in the morning, we would be lucky to get as much sleep as they did then.

The point is clear: Spirituality is not about abusing our bodies. On the contrary. It is about people living a healthy spiritual life that sustains both our spirits and our work. It's about resting so that our spirituality can calm us, quiet us, invigorate us while we do our work well.

Integrating the Practice

Our lives are complex, intense, and sometimes overwhelming. We are a culture on the move. Always. We go from one thing to another day after day: We take care of the baby, get the groceries, work eight hours at the local diner, go to night school to get a degree so we can find a better job, go to the game with the family on the weekend. And all the while, it's the aura of gratitude and the sense of work accomplished and the rest which sustains us that count. At the same time, the commitment to rest as well as to work is what enables us to keep going on with calm and quiet care.

As science identifies the relationship between an undercurrent of holy gratitude and Lauds for us, it has also demonstrated the need for holy rest in our lives. If we are really to develop the spir-

ituality of thanksgiving to which Vespers leads us, we need the rest
that enables us to go on working.

Rest in the Western world—as life gets more and more plagued
by burnout than blessed by achievement—is only now becoming
recognized as the grace we need to sustain the energy we need.
Sleep studies in every major academic psychology project agree
that rest is the major driver of human health and welfare. Doctors
tell us that sleep and rest boost the immune system and actually
protect us physically. We know now that the hormones we need
to be both physically active and mentally alert are developed while
we sleep.

Sleep not only improves memory but enables you to synthe-
size new ideas by integrating old ideas with new ones. Just as important, sleep restores you physically. It repairs tissues, builds
muscles, controls appetite, and monitors sex drive. While you
sleep, the brain stimulates creativity and reduces the stress of forcing production. With rest you become less anxious, less depressed,
while forcing yourself to go on producing does nothing but make
you even more tired. Even moderate sleep, science tells us, is better than no sleep at all, but not enough sleep does slow your responses by 50 percent and leaves you as inaccurate as a person
under the influence of alcohol. Finally, a good sleep regime makes
you happier. It is the single greatest influence on your daily mood.
And with good sleep, you rest in the heart of God, as Benedict
meant for you to do. You find yourself thankful for the challenges,
sure of the energy it takes to go on dealing with the questions,
problems, disappointing failures, and great successes, all of which
invade life with serious regularity.

Sleep keeps you mentally and emotionally fit, able to continue
lifting the weights of life without being crushed by them.

At Vespers, at the last evaluation of the day, we become calm
in the face of darkness, trusting in the face of tomorrow. What has

brought me from Lauds to Vespers will carry me through the
night when I can rise and begin the whole monastic cycle of praise
and thanksgiving, of care, compassion, and concern for the world
around me all over again.

**As science identifies the relationship between an undercurrent
of holy gratitude and Lauds for us, it has also demonstrated
the need for holy rest in our lives. If we are really to develop
the spirituality of thanksgiving to which Vespers leads us, we
need the rest that enables us to go on working.**

26

HOLY LEISURE

On Quality of Life

**Holy leisure, Sabbath time, is the contemplative call
to rest in God's care and at the same time to do our
part to care for the world.**

I have noticed that when I entitle one of my lectures "The Place of Leisure in the Monastic Life," heads turn. What leisure? "I never heard of leisure in religious life," a woman told me as I walked away from the lectern. "That's why I didn't enter," she went on. "I loved everything I knew about the sisters, but I also knew that I'd never make it if all they do is work all the time."

I get the impression that there is another serious misconception about monastic life abroad in the land. So, we need to be direct about this question: Exactly what is the relationship of work to leisure in the Rule of Benedict? Or perhaps an even better way to ask the question is this: Is monastic life nothing but work?

Consider for a moment the amount of time given to each monastic in the daily schedule of the sixth century: In the Rule of Benedict, about four hours a day are allotted for prayer. In fact, that schedule was still a common feature of monastic life when I myself entered the monastery. After the liturgical reform of the

1950s and 1960s, however, the minor Liturgical Hours were either eliminated or condensed to conform to the exigencies of modern life. That change was a good one. It put an end to "getting prayer in" and allowed monasteries the time to give each part of the Divine Office the kind of serious reflection that stretches the soul and so makes every act of life a prayer.

Work is allotted six to nine hours a day, depending on the season and the amount of planting or harvesting to be done.

Finally, reading, study, reflection, and lectio—all private activities—are scheduled for three and a half hours daily at a minimum. Which leaves at least three hours for holy leisure—for development activities and personal growth.

Reading, study, reflection, and lectio are essential elements of a contemplative life. In the mind of Benedict, life is not only lived by working hard and falling into bed facedown-exhausted every night. In fact, his schedules prove that holy leisure—the kind of leisure that settles and shapes the soul—is as much an essential part of Benedictine spirituality as work is. The daily schedule is clear: The monastics work about six to nine hours a day; their prayer, reading, study, reflection, and lectio account for about the same amount of time.

Clearly, Benedictine life is not just about manual labor and saying prayers together. It is also about immersion in thought, consideration of life, an attempt to grow personally and well. Reading, study, reflection, and lectio are the components that make monasticism a serious and thoughtful life, a rich and developing life.

The modern world makes leisure and play synonymous. Benedictinism does not. Real leisure—holy leisure, Sabbath leisure—has more to do with quality of life than it does with play, whose purpose and effect on life are entirely different. Reading a good book by the lake is leisure, is a Sabbath moment that refreshes the soul. Going to a Halloween party is play. The distinction is an important one. Leisure brings us to new heights of understanding and reflection. Play takes us out of thoughtful activity to physical release. It is the Sabbath times of life that take our souls to the heights and leave them there—wiser, deeper, calmer, and happier than any amount of scheduled recreation can ever do.

Judaism shows us the roots of this kind of thinking in our own tradition. From Friday at sundown until Saturday at sundown— Sabbath time—all manual labor stops. In fact, anything that I define as my work, the way I make my living—is suspended. In Jerusalem a rabbi explained it to me this way: "I am a writer and a lecturer," he said. "During Sabbath, I never touch a computer, a television, a mobile phone, or a keyboard. I never give an order to a laborer or respond to a phone call." Then, he took a ballpoint pen out of his jacket, held it up in front of my eyes, twirled it between his fingers, and said, "On the Sabbath I do not carry a pen."

The purpose of Sabbath, the rabbis taught, was threefold: First, to free the poor as well as the rich for at least one day a week. Second, to give people time to evaluate their work as God had evaluated the work of creation to see if their work, too, is life-giving, is good. Finally, Sabbath is meant to give people space to contemplate the real meaning and great questions of life. If anything has brought the modern world to the brink of destruction it must surely be the loss of Sabbath.

Integrating the Practice

The purpose of holy leisure is to bring a kind of spiritual-material balance back into lives gone askew. It's meant to give people time to live thoughtful as well as productive lives. When people sleep in metro stations, it is holy leisure that asks, Why? It is the contemplative reflection of holy leisure that brings us to ask what it is to follow the Gospel in this situation now, in this place here.

When 200,000 soldiers and another 100,000 civilians—most of them children—were exterminated in forty-three days, their land made desolate, and their future "bombed back into the pre-industrial age" in Iraq in 1991, what was really solved? In the face of one of the oldest peoples on the earth, holy leisure asks, How can such a thing be done over and over again in this so-called modern world—and possibly be of God?

When the media asked high-ranking government officials how many Iraqis, as well as Americans, had been killed in Iraq in 2004 and the official answered, "That is a number in which I have no interest whatsoever," it is holy leisure that breaks the secular silence and asks the Sabbath question: *Why not?*

When our environmental rape—air pollution, deforestation, and toxic waste—results in famine, desertification, and poverty around the globe, and doubles the amount of childhood asthma for people who had nothing to do with its causes, it is holy leisure that asks, How did our today became more important than God's tomorrow?

Holy leisure, in other words, is the foundation of contemplation, and contemplation is the ability to see the world as God sees it. Benedictine Dom Cuthbert Butler wrote: "It is not the presence of activity that destroys the contemplative life; it is the absence of contemplation." In Benedictine spirituality, life is not divided into parts holy and mundane. To the monastic mind all of life is holy. All of life's actions bear the scrutiny of all of life's ideals. All of life is to be held in anointed hands.

No, personal comfort, purposeless play, vacuous vacations

have not saved the world. We need the wisdom of holy leisure now. It is our commitment to holy leisure—yours and mine— that is the leadership required in this millennium.

When people sleep in metro stations, it is holy leisure that asks, Why? It is the contemplative reflection of holy leisure that brings us to ask what it is to follow the Gospel in this situation now, in this place here.

27

<hr>

SERVICE

On Caring for Humankind

**Where labor and communal responsibility are concerned, the
Rule of Benedict brooks no doubt, no discussion, no
dilemma: Work of all kind is a basic element of the spiritual
life. "Idleness is the enemy of the soul," Benedict writes in
chapter 48 of the Rule. Sloth is not a monastic virtue, and
caring for one another is the pillar on which it stands.**

The Sayings of the Desert Monastics are wisdom stories from
the deserts of Egypt in the third century that illuminate the
dimensions of a life that most of us only speculate about.

One of their stories is especially relevant to the topic of service. In this tale, it's important to know that the monastics of the
time supported themselves in large part by weaving baskets from
reeds. This leaves a message for our time that sears the soul.

The story reads: "One brother, when he had finished his baskets and put handles on them, heard the monk next door saying,
'What shall I do? The trader is coming and I don't have handles to
put on my baskets.' Then the first brother took the handles off his
own baskets and brought them to his neighbor, saying, 'Look, I
have these left over. Why don't you put them on your baskets?'

And he made his brother's work complete, as there was need, leaving his own unfinished."

This story is a theology of work that has yet to penetrate the hearts of the rest of the world. The truth is that only when the whole community, the whole world is fed and housed and safe is our work really finished on earth. In so many instances, "there is need" that is also our obligation to support.

Benedict's concern in chapter 35 that members should serve one another makes the bridge from personal needs to social consciousness. Benedictines everywhere for fifteen centuries have worked to feed the masses, to save the land, to care for the sick and the poor, to preserve the learnings of humankind, to welcome strangers, to bring beauty to the unsightliness of this world.

The early spiritual masters spoke of acedia as the "demon of the noonday sun." Willingness to simply sit back and let the needs of the world go by is a spiritual disease. It is the doldrums of the soul, in other words. Good work, done well, monasticism teaches, is its only cure. Without it we stand to shrivel and die within ourselves.

At the end of the day, monasticism is not about withdrawing from life for the sake of "wasting time with God," as one new disciple defined it to be. On the contrary. Monastic spirituality and its centuries-old commitment to the land, to art, to hospitality, to learning, to community is, first, a call to service, to human development, to public responsibility. As it is for us now, as well. Our spiritual task is to do something that has value for our own time. Otherwise, why were we born?

Second, being idle is not a synonym for being spiritual. On the contrary. Being spiritual sees where God's work is not being done and moves immediately to fill that gap.

Third, work is cocreative. It develops the worker as well as the work. We are called to recognize our gifts and to give them. Benedictinism is everyone doing their best at what they do best, like the basket maker who gave away his handles so that everyone around him and his neighbor would grow spiritually as well as economically.

Integrating the Practice

The Benedictine tradition teaches you that you do not live off of other people. You work in order to earn your own way through life without burdening those who have their own. You earn your own living as much as you possibly can.

Work, monasticism teaches, is a kind of spiritual asceticism that disciplines you to stay in spiritual shape. To simply let yourself go, to turn into a professional reality-show watcher at an early age, to stop contributing to social projects, to turn to purposeless dust is to allow yourself to disintegrate on all four levels: intellectual, professional, social, and spiritual. All of which makes you deadweight in the society around you. You have wasted yourself for nothing.

Work is about service. You don't work simply for yourself; you work for the good of others both in the monastery—the monastic family—and in the public arena outside of it.

You are also called to work for those who cannot work. You work in order to give alms, to take care of those who need care. You work hard in order to have enough left over to take care of the poor in your midst. By caring for those who need care. By opening a soup kitchen, maybe; by starting a low-cost housing project, perhaps; by working with other groups in order to double your service in the face of what's needed.

Work witnesses to the dignity of labor and of laborers. Societies that rose on the backs of slaves and the poor have created their decrepitude and owe these people both support and opportunities for development. However high your own educational status, however much money you've made, you are not excused from meeting the needs of those society has left behind.

I give. I support. I serve. I do whatever people need and whatever my gifts prepare me to provide. In the end, the monastic charism of work has a history of enriching the world. The history of the Benedictine Order lies in its quiet service to the areas it touches.

Monasticism has been a gift on many levels:

By developing agriculture, monastics reclaimed whole swaths of land in France.

By providing hospitality and hospices, they made European travel safe in unsafe times.

By hand-copying manuscripts, they saved the intellectual legacy of the Greco-Roman world.

By educating entire populations, they raised up generations.

By modeling the integration of work and monastic life itself, they demonstrated how a daily rhythm allows time for community building, time for spiritual and contemplative development, and time for personal development, all three needed to maintain life communally, socially, and individually.

The question for our time is a simple but soul-saving one: Where would my own work fit in the monastic schema? What must I do if I am really to save my world as well as myself? One thing is for sure: The monastic heart does not quit working for the welfare of the world, however prepared I might be to support myself financially. I do not put my feet up and let the rest of the world carry me. Where will you fit into the monastic commit-

ment to continue the work that makes the world the kind of creation the Creator meant for it to be?

**At the end of the day, monasticism is not about withdrawing
from life for the sake of "wasting time with God," as one new
disciple defined it to be. Monastic spirituality is first a call to
service, to human development, to public responsibility.**

28

LISTENING

On Attentiveness

The first word of the Rule of Benedict—a unique and
revolutionary approach to human community in the sixth
century—is Listen.

O f all the chapters in the Rule of Benedict, the Prologue is
surely the most revolutionary, the most prophetic, the most
humanizing. Here's why: It turns the goals of the world upside
down. It takes the position that money and power, oppression and
injustice are no longer the essence of either personal life or the
social order.

Our ways are not the ways, the values, the goals of the world.
The Rule is clear. It reads, "Is there anyone here who yearns for life
and desires to see good days?" Then, not a hint of money or power,
control or status, public acclaim or social achievement. Instead,
the answer comes back: "If you hear this and your answer is 'I do,'
God then directs these words to you: If you desire true and eternal
life, 'keep your tongue free from vicious talk and your lips from all
deceit; turn away from evil and do good; let peace be your quest
and aim.'"

Remember that this Rule was written at the beginning of the
sixth century, a time of empires and emperors, of hierarchs and

commoners, of serfs and slaves, of plebeians and patricians, of pilgrims and pillagers. The society in which this Rule was written, in other words, was one in which each dimension of it was clearly defined and socially controlled. At the core of every segment of society loomed the overlordship of the paterfamilias, the oldest living male in a household. It was a title that had serious implications for everyone in every family, every worker on every estate, every person in the empire. All property, all monies, all business decisions, all control on all levels began and ended in the hands of one person in the Roman family. The paterfamilias exercised autocratic authority over the entire estate. In his hands lay the power of life and death over the whole family and all its servants. He was the law there, not to be questioned, not to be opposed.

It's through that filter of blind obedience that the Prologue of the Rule of Benedict must be read. It's knowing how ancient rights structured family life that lets us see how this explanation of monastic life is a revolutionary document. It begins, "Listen carefully, my daughter/son, to my instructions, and attend to them with the ear of your heart."

This Rule is not written in the language of military obedience or as a declaration of canons and commandments. There are no threats defined and no punishments—no dismissal, no debasement, no demands for deference—for those who fail. Instead, the seeker is asked to listen. To evaluate. To respond.

It has taken centuries to realize the implications of the difference between obedience as it has been defined in military modes and listening as the Latin core of the word *obedire* requires. Obedience, in the sense of laying down my personhood at the door, does not seriously begin to disappear until the nineteenth century: Then, suddenly—in the face of the Enlightenment, with its enthronement of the individual; industrialization, which created an organized working class at the mercy of the rich; and compulsory education, which made the underclass as potentially effective as those who inherited, rather than earned, their place in society— society turned inside out.

First, commoners resisted classism, then workers turned to labor unions to balance the power in labor negotiations, then women insisted on civil rights, and by the end of the twentieth century, children had begun to sue their parents! The world and all its superstructures were beginning to topple. Until now.

The spirituality of creation taught us that the God who made us, made us all equal, all competent, and all responsible for the development of life. Which implied that the working class contributed as much to the success of the rich as the rich themselves. Which defied the whole mythos of classism, of the divine authority of authority figures, of racial inferiority, of sexism, and of the very ideas of power and authority themselves.

So now what? In the monastery, the Rule's elimination of autocracy, inferiority, slavery, oppression, and hierarchy began, a step at a time, to erode the entire social system upon which, until then, an individual's place in the world depended. The paterfamilias, one legal move after another, melted away in the mist of a new world in ascendance. Now listening—not submitting to authority—became the name of the game. A game in which everyone held the same divine chips, at least to begin with.

Rights and responsibilities have taken their place in the spiritual vocabulary as well as in the political one. What does that do to obedience as a vow, a virtue, a place in the category of sanctity?

Integrating the Practice

In our lifetime, the psychological community, the medical community, even the business community have come to understand that we can't force-feed ideas to any class of people. "Listening" has allowed people to take in new information, think about it, and make their own choices. People of every rank have begun to give serious consideration to the life path they are about to plod, its moral depth, its social impact, its effect on the planet. The question What am I going to do with my life and why? has become central. Even more important, the question What is a happy life? becomes at least as important as How much money will I make?

Indeed, listening is a spiritual discipline, a step toward full moral maturity, a parallel path to the demands of tradition tried and true. To listen and be listened to, the Rule of Benedict assures us, is an invitation to rethink what we have always thought to be absolute but now know, thanks to the experience and honesty of others, must be rethought. When the rest of the world thinks differently, and I pause to hear why, that is the beginning of conversion of life, of metanoia. It is also the beginning of peace on the planet and fullness of life for everyone. Listening also enables us to explore life through someone else's eyes. It is another link in the chain of personal growth.

If listening leads to learning, it also leads to attentiveness to others. Having known pain, you can walk with others through theirs, without judgment, without disdain, without diminishing the feelings that underlie the suffering of others. Even more important, listening to another stands to change your own perspectives on life. It challenges your assumptions and sends you away thinking more deeply about what it means to be fully alive. It demonstrates how dangerous it is to be absolutist about anything.

In the Prologue of Benedict's Rule you discover that your obedience is to the will of God, not to any lesser authority. The Rule, written fifteen centuries ago, does not chain you to itself. It tells you to listen, to weigh what the times demand, rather than what the past demanded. It frees you to listen to the world, to others, to the needs of the time, to the issues around you, to new ideas and to old wisdom that never staled, never withered, never failed the world. Then, you are free from old ideas for oldness's sake. Now you are able to judge old systems, old taboos, old control figures in order to live an ancient life newly.

Then, you have obeyed the Rule by listening for the will of God for this time, in you, always. The revolution of rights has been protected by monasticism, the prophetic spirit is still alive, the call to personal growth has been accomplished through the centuries.

Listening to another stands to change our own perspectives on life. It challenges our assumptions and sends us away thinking more deeply about what it means to be fully alive. It demonstrates how dangerous it is to be absolutist about anything.

29

PRIVATE PRAYER

On God and Self

**The space designated as the prayer center of the community
is an open invitation to monastics to take the opportunity for
time, space, and quiet to center their lives in God.**

The designation of prayer space, tone, and atmosphere softens
and opens the human heart. It is the necessary setting for
personal spiritual growth.

The spiritual life and the writing life are two pieces of the same
soul. It took a long time for me to understand that, but do both
for a while and you will find it difficult to distinguish one from
the other. In fact, maybe there isn't any distinction at all.

The sole writing teacher I ever had taught only five things. He
said that to be a writer five practices were necessary: (1) Write in
the same place every day; (2) Write at the same time every day;
(3) Write the same amount of time every day; (4) If the words do
not flow, sit there and stare at the paper or screen till the designated period of time is over, then return the next day to try again;
and (5) Never, ever, let anybody read what you have written until
it's finished, otherwise the bubbles will go off the champagne.

Then he looked the ten of us straight in the eye and ended by saying, "That is everything I can teach you about writing. Now it's up to you: Get out of here and do it."

The principles were basic. They were also very precise.

By identifying a certain place in which to write every day, I am setting up a kind of trigger to creativity. My mind knows that when I sit down in this room and this chair, it is time to write. Only write. Nothing else.

By deciding the time at which I will write every day, I am committing myself to one task and concentrating on one task only for this prescribed period.

By promising that I will write for a defined amount of time every day, I put myself under the urgency to produce something. Now and here. Not someday, somewhere.

By allowing ideas to well up in me spontaneously, I am refusing to give up when the ideas don't come or trying to force ideas that are still embryos within me. Now I am contemplating in order to get ready to write.

By refusing to share my writing with others before it is finished, I am allowing creativity to take over rather than adopt someone else's ideas. I am making my writing my own.

It is interesting to see that what that process taught me about writing has affected my spiritual life deeply. The kind of concentration and commitment the writing process teaches is a walk into another world. Only this time it is a walk into the spiritual world I have been trying to contact for years. It is the world into which the Rule of Benedict sends us when it tells us to practice private prayer.

Integrating the Practice

Indeed, I learned a lot about more than writing that day. I learned about harnessing concentration. I began to realize the kind of creativity that it takes to focus, to clarify spiritual concepts. I learned to listen to my unconscious self, to the questions, concerns, and calls of the life I was living. I learned what it really means to listen.

What's more, I learned more about the superstructure of the spiritual life from my writing teacher in that seminar than I ever did in the novitiate. I didn't really figure that out, I admit, until I had immersed myself in the Rule for years. And, specifically, in chapter 52, "The Oratory of the Monastery." It was a chapter that seemed out of place and, to my younger self, relatively useless. Why write a chapter about a single room in a monastery? Then one day I finally got it. The oratory—the chapel—the very center of our lives, a sacred place, is a place set apart to enable us, when we go there, to sink into God.

Then I realized that all the great things of life, the holy things, the deep and restless and uncertain parts of our souls need our full concentration. Such conundrums need serious reflection and our deepest attention. They need time to grow; they need regular, steady, daily presence. They need to be free from outside distractions. They need a place where we can go and just sit and wait for the Word to move our souls, to touch our hearts, to center our lives. "Let the oratory be what it is called," the Rule says of the chapel, "and nothing else is to be done or stored there."

Those teachings crystallize our minds:

Defined times for prayer and reflection provide the psychological parameters of our lives. What we give time to is what we are or what we want to become. We practice musical instruments, we read one book after another, we take a walk before we start the day, we spend family time together every day, every week, every summer, every holiday. The effect of it all is definitive. What we give time to creates us.

Private space, solitude—the earthly heaven of the hermit— waits within the heart of all of us to expose us to our deepest selves. It's space that frees us from the distractions of the world. It insulates us; it walls us away from the minutiae of the day. It releases the rest of us to ourselves.

Virginia Woolf, one of the outstanding writers of the twentieth century, one of the few women writers of the time, underscored the need for space as the soul of human development. Few women were professional writers, she pointed out, not because they could not write but because they had no space of their own in which to write. Men had offices; women had kitchens. No houses identified parlors for women to retire to in order to think about life as they did dens for men. There were no private desks for women; no private rooms where they could go to think, to be alone, to work without interruption, to pray, to wrestle with the psalms, to find the God who waits there.

Silence drains the mind of the peripherals of life. It wipes the slate of the heart clean of the agitation, the fragmented memories, the extraneous. It clears your mind. It allows you to sweep away whatever enables you to hide from the things that are worrying you, irritating you, frightening you. Then, secure in the space and free of the demands of time you may relax into the silence of God, where no words are necessary and no feelings are barred.

What I learned in a writing seminar about the importance of time and space and silence to the writing process and the development of the writer's mind brought flesh and blood to the spiritual life as well. It made clear to me in ways nothing else could that chapter 52 of the Rule, on the oratory, means to give us the time and space and silence and solitude we need to become spiritual as well as religious in a way no one had ever done before.

To become truly, spiritually mature, Benedict tells us here, we must take what we learn in choral prayer—at Lauds and Vespers, in the scriptures and hymns of the great feasts—to our inner selves. Regularly, deeply, silently, privately until, finally, we become what we say we are. We must practice our spiritual life in real space and time. We must make the oratory what it is called: the place we go to listen to the Spirit within.

We are called to create a private relationship with the God with whom we have a public one. Yes, we go to prayers always and regularly. Yes, we are part of the community choir that prays the psalms aloud for all the world to hear. But we are also called to make what we pray in chapel the centerpiece of our lives. We are able in our little oratories to give our lives over to a personal relationship with the God who lives within us, waiting for us to attend to it. Privately, honestly, and also regularly.

It's a simple reality that we manage to make complex as we go. Instead, we turn God into a child's myth. We make God a warrior, a magician, a vending machine, a judge, the remote puppeteer of the universe. And all the time, Benedict shows us, God waits for us in the oratory of our hearts, awaiting our attention to the only thing that really matters in life: that we find our Creator God who is also looking for us.

To paraphrase what the professor said, "That's all that can be taught about the truly spiritual life: Find a space where you can concentrate; take the time every day to rest in God there; stay at it however elusive it may seem on some days; let the ideas come and, if you do these things, you will find your way to the Spirit who is awaiting you within you. Then you will build a relationship with God that is life-changing. Yours."

Then, chapter 52 is clear. It says without artifice, "Get out of here and do it."

We must practice our spiritual life in real space and time. We must make the oratory what it is called: the place we go to listen to the Spirit within.

30

OBEDIENCE

On Mutuality

Obedience is one of the three vows or lifelong promises
Benedictines make to mark their lasting commitment to
the order. Obedience commits a sister to allegiance to the
Rule of Benedict and the Prioress as the basis for both
individual and communal decisions that shape all the
dimensions of Benedictine life.

Benedictine life is not a life of rugged individualism. Neither is it a life of childish dependence. It is life lived on a straight line between personal conscience and community development. The major obligation of both the community and the individual is not simply to preach the Gospel but to live it—here, now, as a community and as an individual of conscience.

There are those who shudder at the thought of being accountable to anyone but themselves. On the other hand, there are those who are independent enough to know that total independence is both impossible and dangerous. It is total independence that leads us to make reckless or impetuous decisions without counsel, without discernment, without direction. It leaves us on our own when we most need the insights and experience of others.

In Benedictine monasteries, wisdom and experience are the

building blocks on which the community stands. The great decisions are made by the group itself. Should the community take on debt to provide housing for the elderly? Maybe. Should the community take a public stand on behalf of the rights of women, for instance? Yes, but how? To resolve major questions like that in a group is a holy act of trust and genuine community.

At the same time, obedience is even more: It is an act of trust in one another's obedience to the movement of the Spirit among us. It levels the group and makes everyone's responses equally important. It's not about force; it's about enabling everyone to add to the decisions, to consider life carefully, to move thoughtfully.

It means that the Benedictine vow of obedience does not discard either a person's free will or a person's obligation to pursue the knowledge it will take to make informed decisions. It does not bind a person to a blind future or to a meaningless life. Instead, the Benedictine vow of obedience promises a person the safety net of wisdom.

The Prioress holds the Rule in one hand and the needs of the community in the other. She sharpens our sense of the broader needs outside ourselves. She refuses to allow us to become a world unto ourselves. She stretches our public presence by calling us into something greater than we could ever have thought ourselves capable of doing. She is the wisdom figure of the tradition who keeps our hearts attuned to the impact of Benedictinism before our age and alive to our obligation to have an effect on our own.

Benedictine obedience, however, stretches further than the Prioress. Community life itself affords the kind of spiritual companionship that comes from the experience of those who have lived life years before us and know life's dark sides in ways we have yet to discover. They give us the strength and confidence it takes to strike out again in our own era as they did before it. Otherwise, too many freeze on life's path—afraid to move on, unwilling to try—just when we should obey the Gospel call and give our public selves to it again.

And the proof of all that is? Easy. Obedience is about the interdependence and spiritual companionship that points the community forward in the same spirit that drove it in the past.

Integrating the Practice

When the Rule was written fifteen centuries ago, the word *obedience,* contrary to contemporary usage, did not mean to conform as it does now. *Obedience—obedire*—meant to listen. As the Prologue of the Rule says, obedience is an invitation, not a command. "Listen carefully, my daughter/son," it says, not "Obey me when I tell you to do something."

In that very subtle but very important difference is the foundation of human relationships. Therein lies the whole secret to life in a monastery and life in a marriage, to life on the job and life on our different journeys through life, to life as a parent or teacher and life as a leader or well-loved guide. It's the kind of listening you do that counts. On both sides.

Our generation is finally beginning to realize how damaging it can be to make people conform rather than to enable them to discover their own gifts, their own sense of purpose, and the new growth a new challenge can bring.

Life decisions in a marriage, once based on legislation that made the wife subject to the husband, have now become an exercise in mutuality. Now both partners know what's going on. The husband and wife who do not listen to one another, who do not make decisions together, will not long sustain a real marriage. Anything else, we know now, is not a partnership built on the care and sensitivity and support of each other. It's little more than legal captivity.

Children whose ideas are overlooked, whose desires are ignored, whose questions are suppressed, whose hopes are demeaned are sure to rebel before it's over. Worse, they leave home untutored in decision-making, unaware of their real abilities, grossly undeveloped both emotionally and socially.

Attending to the rights and responsibilities of all is the way a family either learns from one another or lapses into the kind of alienation that divides people who should love one another most. It's the way a government either learns from the people or faces its collapse. It's the way spiritual leaders grow with the learnings of the culture around them or become leaders of a cult rather than of a faith.

It is respect for the ideas of others that eliminates both the dependence of blind obedience, which corrodes a person's own insights, and authoritarianism, which cripples the group's development.

Discovering the needs of society is what makes it possible for people of faith to do for the world what the world most needs now. In the 1850s the world needed education, and most religious orders began schools and religious themselves became teachers. Then, over time, it became clear that what the world really needed now was soup kitchens, and free medical clinics, and adult literacy courses, and childcare, and counseling centers and art therapy, and acceptance of the equality of women in both church and state—as well as more schools. It was out of that mutual concern that religious obeyed what they saw as the call of the Gospel in a new era and so became new themselves.

The question for you and me now, as both lay and religious, is To what do we listen most in life? To the need to get more money? To the desire to control others? To the attempt to get our own way, regardless of the needs of others?

In being accountable to our talents, to our conscience, and to our call to obey the will of God for the people we serve is the ultimate fidelity to the vow of obedience. It is through the monastic vow of obedience, of listening, that both lay and religious touch the world now as those who made that promise have done in every era since the sixth century. The monastic heart listens and by listening obeys the will of God for us all.

It is total independence that leads us to make reckless or impetuous decisions without counsel, without discernment, without direction. It leaves us on our own when we most need the insights and experience of others. Listening is about enabling everyone to add to the decisions, to consider life carefully, to move thoughtfully.

31

STABILITY

On Perseverance

The vow of stability, another of the Benedictines' three lifelong commitments, calls seekers to complete the path they
have begun. "Even when hard things are commanded," the
Rule says, "persist and do not grow weary."

B enedict tells us that stability in a community of spiritual companions calls us to grow to the fullness of ourselves. No one
knows us better than the people we have lived and worked next to
every day of our adult lives. They know our selfishness, our little
irritations, our barely concealed resentments and criticism. We
can't hide them or deny them where we are, as we can when we
move from place to place, stranger to stranger. We can pretend to
holiness then. But to achieve real holiness, Benedict teaches us, we
must realize that emotional stability is the attitude of heart that
brings us to learn from life—rather than bolt from its stings. The
ability to endure and grow, he says, enriches everything we do.
Most of all, perseverance is a process of maturation. One that is
learned, but slowly. Only stability can offer that kind of honesty,
of soulful growth.

Life, Benedict says, needs to be lived with those who cannot
only help us grow but also help us to control, to soften, to trans-

form our rough edges into gifts. His position is clear: It's easy to leave a community when it demands that we grow up. But the rush to freedom at the moment of accountability is at best an escape, not a justification; it is self-centered, not wise.

The really important thing to understand is that monasticism is not an efficient system; it is a patient one, however. It is about growth, not conformity. The dilemma is that growth is slow. Everywhere. In everything. Grass takes time to grow. Trees take months to blossom. And we're like that, too. Worse, understanding our need to grow also comes slowly. To realize the import of what life is about we must live it—accept it—consciously and to its core.

To feel the pain that comes with death and empties our lives of friends, of family, of love and support, to deal with that kind of suffering and the fear of the future, to face collapse in the face of stress takes great internal strength. And yet all these are essential if we are to live full and rich lives. We must be open to multiple experiences because every experience, distilled, develops in us another level of insight. Then, emotionally balanced in our sensibilities, open to lifelong learning, contentment sets in at the end. We know now that we can bear life in all its dimensions.

The inner energy that guides us up one hill after another in life is called stability. It is about staying at this enigma called development, whatever its challenges. We are not born prepared for every test and trial life has to offer. In each of them is the hidden growth we either think we don't need or know we don't want. But if we grow through these trials, life teaches us, we will create a life that is truly rich, genuinely serene.

We come to fullness of life in stages: First the body develops, then the mind engages with the world, then the heart begins to feel, then the soul starts to reflect on it all. It can take years. That's why living till we die—being willing to go on learning all the way to the end—takes a great deal of emotional balance. To be amenable, to continue working through all the dimensions of life till we see their value for us is the essence of spiritual maturity. This is how stability—the capacity for dealing with all the dimensions of life in an equitable and reasonable manner—becomes such an important dimension of development. We learn in high school the math that powers nuclear bombs, for instance. But it can be years before we finally fathom the extent, the impact, the sinfulness of their use.

We meet someone we're sure we love and discover five years later that it wasn't love at all. It was attraction grounded in chemistry rather than mutuality and values and common vision. Even more important, each of us goes through this development, this awareness, alone. No one can give it to us. Which itself takes a great deal of stability to accept.

Nevertheless, the place of stability in life is a relatively new concept. It took fifteen centuries for science and psychology to realize what Benedict already knew, that neuroticism—emotional instability, negativity, personal inquietude, perpetual restlessness— threatens the very foundations of life.

The vows he asked of monastics are clear about that: He wanted us to listen to wisdom figures. He wanted us to pursue the transformation of our struggling selves in the here and now. He wanted us to pursue union with God as our foremost intention. He wanted us to trust monastic life to bring us out whole and holy in body and soul. He wanted us to see that it is the health of the soul that enables us to brave whatever environment we live in.

And all of that takes a lifetime.

What could be more important in this day and age?

Integrating the Practice

Our society feeds on change. And the way we address it makes all the difference. Americans, we're told, don't save money much anymore. Apparently, they simply expect it to come to them. Even keeping a job is not very important in our generation. Guidance counselors now advise that people have at least four positions on their résumés to be considered valuable to the professional world. Something else will come along, we say. There will be dull seasons, yes, but we can simply leave and try again. The very notion of working through an issue, a problem—even a marriage—has become foreign to us. So much for the psychological value of stability.

Yet all the while, the inner person is crumbling. There has been no acquired sense of success, of working on a project until it's completed. Endurance is not a quality of life. Patient perseverance has become more an irritant than a mark of strength. Waiting is not acceptable. Winning is not a skill to be developed, slowly, slowly until you are really in charge of who you are and what you do. Instead, breakdown—the sense of hopelessness and failure—has come to be expected. Except that when what you want doesn't happen, the temptation that grips the soul is to simply step off the ladder of life, curl up in a corner, and quit. "I tried" becomes momentary rather than a way of life.

The effect of that approach on your life and success is spiritual bankruptcy. You forget that, however naturally talented the musician, the fruits of that talent can't be achieved without practice. Intense and daily and long-term, lifetime practice. You, on the other hand, are in an instant coffee world. You want life on a platter. Now. Which is where the monastic mind approaches the world differently. Monastics do not so much live to achieve—and therefore dissolve emotionally if it does not happen—as to strive for what is possible, so that, little by little, the world can achieve what it seeks. Happiness, monasticism teaches you, belongs to those who are emotionally stable enough to bear the present in order to reap the future.

Indeed, stability is the bedrock of every generation. To skip from challenge to challenge, meeting few if any of them, can only throw your life into perpetual disarray. It is stability that carries you over the hard places of life. It protects you from the psychic negativity that eats away inside you, at your very sense of self. Having weeded out the negativity that has plagued us is exactly what makes looking at life with good humor, with steady trust, possible.

Stability keeps you on your feet when it feels as if the world around you has buried you in pain. Until you can hardly breathe. Then it is stability that whispers, "Stop." It saves you from the cataract of feelings that threatens to overwhelm you. It saves you from giving up when what you want does not come.

Only when it's over—when you have learned to try, to wait as long as it takes, to get help rather than simply walk out on the project, to apologize for being emotionally excitable, unreasonable—will you ever come to realize that life is lived in years, not in minutes; in wind and waves, not on the leeward side of life. Then, when stress does come, as it surely will, you are ready to live it through, to be positive, to be happy, to face life without fear, without disintegrating emotionally. You will have become stable and so can help make life stable for others.

What is really at issue, contemporary psychology knows now, is not how bad the situation is but how much of yourself you have brought to living it well. To live a stable life in the monastic spirit is to take responsibility for your world as it is. It is about bringing the peace, spreading the love, and putting your shoulders to the task of steadying life as it is and making life as it should be. To those whose hearts are stable only one thing is clear: When the smoke swirls and the rain drives and the winds whip up again, we will all still be standing. What you do to bring calm and care to others will make all the difference to life as you know it.

The things you believe, the attitudes that burn within you, the images of life and people you harbor and hold, the thoughts you think can all be changed. By whom? By you.

Human beings take a lot of time to come to wholeness—but, eventually, if you are willing, come to wholeness you will. Unfortunately, it never happens all at once. Which is what stability is all about. Hang on. It's worth it.

To live till we die—being willing to go on learning all the way to the end—takes a great deal of emotional balance. To be amenable, to continue working through all the dimensions of life till we see their value for us is the essence of spiritual maturity.

32

PEACE AND JUSTICE

On Peacemaking

Pax, the Latin for peace, is the official motto of Benedictine
life. Benedictine Pax has two facets: one personal,
the other global. The two are closely related.

The first dimension of Benedictine peace is a commitment to
personal calm and serenity—a gift of aplomb to a complex
and agitated world. This kind of peace brings a sense of equanimity and patience to those most harried by life forever at warp
speed.

The second dimension of Benedictine peace has to do with
peacemaking itself, with the way we ourselves face pressure, sometimes even danger, in a world of opposites, of strangers, of those
who are not "our kind of people."

Pax has a long and ironic history. The early use of this term
may be one of the first times in the Western world when one
group became consciously absorbed by the language that de-
scribed another—and turned that initial meaning upside down.

The first widespread use of the term was applied not to monastics but to Roman life. Pax Romana, the term given to the rule of
Rome between 27 B.C. and A.D. 180, defines an almost two-
hundred-year period when all the countries around the Mediter-

ranean were united under the Roman Empire. This pax, however, was an unnatural peace that looked good for a while but deteriorated under its own weight. Rome's legions, which maintained the peace in areas distant from Rome, were overextended and too costly to sustain, so the empire collapsed financially. Rome was a hollow master, but a master nonetheless. The Pax Romana became a shell of an idea based on an unnatural system—wealth, war, power, control, and suppression of peoples. None of its pillars were fully human, none of them reflected the will of God for all people. None of them could last in the face of other ambitious and militaristic societies.

With the decline of Rome, Europe became a cavalcade of chaos. Average laborers had no jobs, no money, no security. Life was all about what people could get for themselves, and what they could manage to maintain. With no central government left, small landowners fought for power one inch of turf at a time. Then monastic communities stepped in; they established judicial systems, they heard complaints, they arbitrated differences, they gave spiritual direction. They became the centers of the social system. They kept the peace.

But there were bigger problems. All of Europe was a hive of conflict. With the breakdown of government, the whole notion of the "Royal Peace" disintegrated for lack of support. This compact among members of the ruling class of the ninth century, which declared that the weak of society—especially ecclesiastical properties, women, priests, pilgrims, and merchants—would be spared the terrors of war, was no longer honored.

Monastics, too, were immersed in these negotiations. Benedictines were key to promoting peace as a spiritual value as well as a social need. Most of all, this ideal not only contributed to the stabilization of the eleventh century but laid the basis for a new kind of public contract. It seeded a newly emerging awareness that the community itself needed to give aid to the poor and protect the defenseless if human life was going to be humane for everyone. Modern European peace movements still owe a great deal to these early insights and efforts.

Benedictines were central, as well, to the development of the Truce of God, another major social attempt to stop violence so that communities could concentrate on development rather than survival. This time various warring factions agreed to outlaw fighting on specific days and times. This agreement prohibited fighting from 9:00 P.M. Saturday to 3:00 A.M. Monday. Fighting was later prohibited from Wednesday evening to Monday morning in addition to religious feast days. That left only eighty days a year for fighting. By 1123, violation of the calendar of violence carried the threat of excommunication, and by the thirteenth century the rise of strong national governments made such individual commitments unnecessary.

Monastic life was a life without weapons, in a world full of warlords and sieges. Even monasteries that themselves fell to the onslaught of foreign tribes did not fight back.

Finally, monastics were highly instrumental in forging peace among the warring lords of every region. The role of monasticism in the search for peace left enduring cultural marks. The Peace of God and the Truce of God, which imposed controls on the conduct of war, led eventually to the concept of the Just War. It guided Christian soldiers to fight only at acceptable times, to protect noncombatants, to make and keep the peace between tribes. It raised the commitment to war to a growing consciousness of the need to separate warriors from innocents—a concept that has only recently been ignored.

Monasticism remained the one enduring commitment to peace in a world where peace lay in the hands of warring forces.

Integrating the Practice

If we are to create global community in our time, there must be a voice that can transcend the current politics and national ambitions.

During the great nuclear buildups of the 1960s, monastics spoke out, organized programs, and raised their voices again and again against national violence as a foundation for human development. Now, with new American threats to deploy nuclear weapons on other peoples, Benedictine peace groups have steadfastly opposed their government's willingness to use lethal force on civilians, to strike first, to prepare for global mayhem, to risk the existence of the planet with their so-called inhuman defense plans.

But what is that to you and me? Just this: Every moment of social tension needs a peacemaker. Otherwise, how can the human family get beyond the competition, domination, annihilation, and blind struggles for power that pass as defense even now? The truth is that only one thing can really bring peace: the commitment that we will not destroy other people's sense of self, of dignity, of value in the name of truth.

Modern Benedictines have gone to the poorest, least educated, most ignored people in the world in order to be voices for the voiceless. Modern-day Benedictines began Benedictines for Peace in a nuclear world. Benedictines of our time have taken corporate commitments to nuclear disarmament and begun new monasteries in the least stable parts of the world.

The commitment to be peace, to speak peace, to create peace wherever you go is the call of monastic peacemakers. Monastic peacemaking illuminates an important distinction between military peace and Benedictine peace. Peace is not an unwillingness to tell a hard truth. It is a commitment not to make war on either the personal or the planetary level in the name of making peace. Peacemaking is your promise to tell truth kindly, clearly, and compassionately. Compassionately.

When you live that promise out, then you are truly peacemakers.

Every moment of social tension needs a peacemaker. Otherwise, how can the human family get beyond the competition, domination, annihilation, and blind struggles for power that pass as defense even now? The truth is that only one thing can really bring peace: the commitment not to destroy other people's sense of self, of dignity, of value in the name of truth.

33

CHANT

On the Sound of Angels

Chant is a monastic prayer form that either recites or sings simple verses of psalms and prayers with rhythm, reiteration of ideas, and fluid musical tones. It ranges from simple psalm tones called plain chant to complex polyphonic Gregorian chant.

"I looked in Temples, Churches and Mosques but I found the Divine within my heart," the Islamic poet Rumi writes. I know the truth of that awareness. I have lived wrapped in the middle of it for more than sixty-five years. More interesting than that, perhaps, is the way that awareness came to me.

It was 1952. I was sixteen years old and wrestling with whether the attraction I felt to monastic life was a real vocation or an adolescent fascination. It was 5:00 P.M. I was leaving campus after a couple hours' work on the high school newspaper.

I came out the back door of the academy and turned to say my usual night prayer at the Marian shrine. Just as I arrived at the statue, the stained-glass windows on the second floor above me opened. Then the sweetest sound I'd ever heard came wafting out of those windows as it had so many times since I'd come to that school. The psalm tone was a haunting one and the singing of it lilting, clear, gentle, and soothing.

The sisters were chanting Matins, the longest of the Liturgical Hours of prayer, which was often said at night "in preparation" rather than at 5:00 A.M. on a school day. I stood stock-still and listened. And I knew. I belonged in this community.

The chanting had done what chanting is meant to do. It raises the mind and heart to God. It elevates consciousness beyond the prosaic and the earthly. It separates us from one kind of world and introduces us to another: the one that probes the soul rather than the mind. The one that settles us into the direction of our lives. The one that shapes our souls and trains the ears of our hearts to hear the spirit of life within us. The one that turns our feet from the path of the popular to the path of human purpose.

All the great traditions—Hinduism, Buddhism, Christianity, Native American tribes, Jewish liturgical music, the Islamic reading of the Koran and the mystical Sufi experience, among others, all use chant to express the deepest understanding of their spiritual ideals.

Chant is not where anyone goes to argue theology or contest the existence of miracles. Chant is where we go to *be*. To simply be that other part of ourselves that tugs at our feet on the ground and raises us up somewhere above them.

Integrating the Practice

Chant deepens the very nature of prayer. Its purpose is not to distract you from prayer, from the very depth of your soul, as do so many other things in life. Not as do your concerns about the schedule for the day with all its irritations or the need to rush breakfast to get to a meeting in town.

And the very nature of the feast days of the Church raises the plane of chant from the range of simple monotones to a level of complex, polyphonic Gregorian chant, which is centuries old yet new every day of your life. It's this chant that encapsulates the prayer, that insulates you from meaningless noise around you. It makes heaven a place near you and a part of the ether of life.

At the same time, chant makes prayer a sharper, clearer human event. In chant there is none of the straggling you hear in most prayer recitations, when some of the group start the next line too soon and the others end it too late. Chant makes you literally of one heart. It picks you up and carries you on the waves of the psalm tone and its rhythm into another whole world. It allows you to see what life can be if you are willing to let go of disruptions and take on the quiet, calming flow that chant creates in us.

Chant is a tool of prayer, a servant of the spirit, a sound that blocks out all other sounds you know. Chant captures the words of the heart on a crest of sound that immerses you in the presence of God. Here and now. Nothing else. Just the dialogue of the heart, in which you hear the Word of God in the psalter and respond to it in the center of your own soul. Chant is the universal language of what community is meant to be. Because chanting is done together, you and I are growing into one body. We are giving the world a model of inclusion, of common search, of genuine support.

From a very pragmatic posture, chant becomes a tool of public and personal meditation as well. Its gentle repetition of basic ideas, of the cries of the soul, gets said aloud, touches all of us at once, and calls us evenly and equally into the community of God.

Chant is a very simple, piercing, repetitive, memory-making moment. Its smooth, consistent return to the memory of God's ongoing care for humankind makes straight the path of life for us. We trusted God in the past, we remember every day, and were saved. We trust God now and know, as a result, that we shall not be abandoned. We trust God for the future because we have experienced the love of God before.

Monastics chant over and over again from day to day: "O God, come to my assistance; O God, make haste to help me." This is the antiphon that opens the chanting of the 150 psalms, which will be recited over and over again every week of our lives. Then, eventually, it becomes the beat of the heart, the hope of the seeker. It is the etching of the presence of God on the mind that goes on forever and can never, ever, be forgotten. It is the daily memory and promise of God's presence that clasps two souls to one another: I to God, God to me. It is the sound of the presence of God that never goes away.

In the end, chanting quiets the mind. It opens the heart to contemplation. It takes you down the deep stairs to the cave of the heart and leaves you there to realize the great things God is doing, has done, and will continue to do forever. Chanting moves you into a sense of oneness with the universe, where no thinking or problem-solving is the price of your admission, only awareness of the eternal presence of God, yet new every day of your life.

Chant is a very simple, piercing, repetitive, memory-making moment. Its smooth, consistent return to the memory of God's ongoing care for humankind makes straight the path of life for us. We trusted God in the past, we remember every day, and were saved. We trust God now and know, as a result, that we shall not be abandoned. We trust God for the future because we have experienced the love of God before.

34

INCENSE

On the Sweet Balm of Life

Judeo-Christian rituals and liturgies have used incense for thousands of years as a symbol of the connection between heaven and earth and the harmony of the universe.

When the thurifer, holding the censer, led the procession down the aisle, the smoke streaming, the perfume of it sharp and pervasive, I knew even as a child that life was changing somehow. There was nothing left that was mundane or meaningless. This was pay-attention time. And I did.

But the truth is that incense had been doing this for centuries. In the Jewish tradition, incense was burned on an incense altar every morning and every night. Villagers said they could smell the incense of the Temple as far away as Jericho. The Temple was the seat of power to be honored. It was the incensing of the Temple that made its divine role plain. Only in the Temple could anyone be assured, as the incense burned its sweet way toward heaven, of a connection with the Divine.

Maimonides, the twelfth-century Jewish philosopher-rabbi, explained the function of the incense this way: The sweet incensing of the Temple not only carried the prayers of the people to God but affirmed the very presence of God among us and the obligation of the people to respond. The incensing ritual, he explained, symbolized that the Creator does hear our prayers, that we are under the protection of God.

So important was the incense ritual that the recipe for the incense is, to this day, a secret, a holy act, and the mixing of it can be done only by priests from the Tribe of Aaron. Nor can it be used for domestic purposes.

Christianity—and all the other great religious traditions as well—has given incense a special place in ritual and prayer. Why? Custom only or choice? Clearly, religion has known for a long time what science can only now confirm: that there is a commonality, a universal harmony, a unity in creation. We all come from the same substance; we live under the same laws. As Maimonides explains the Jewish tradition: "All from God; all for God"—or in other language, "All things are sacred; the sacred is in all things."

In Benedictine monasticism, those understandings of the essential holiness of life are also still symbolized by incense. The Nativity story of scripture recounts that the three foreign sages who found the Christ Child came offering gifts: frankincense, to protect the space; and myrrh, to ward off evil. Both these types of incense, incidentally, were far more valuable than their third gift, the gold. It is incense that marks off space in the heavens to connect the presence of God on earth.

But science knows now, too, that incense is a great deal more than simply a symbol of peace, a gesture of purification and the upward rise of our hopes and prayers. It touches a dimension of life that gives us the consciousness and the calm we need to continue the long road to wholeness, through all the darkness, above all the pettiness of life, to its purest, most pointed spirit. Brain studies support the long-held understanding that the burning of incense calms the nervous system, dissipates negative energy, and brings rest to anxiety and stress, harmony to the soul, mindfulness

to meaning, focus to thought, and, of course, a gateway to meditation. Aromatherapy has become a commonplace in modern life.

Incense never goes away. It was an ancient sign before us and
remains a special balm now. It prepares us to recognize and realize
that our lives are made of both dust and stars. And we are to live
in both.

Integrating the Practice

As incense pulls you beyond the ordinary, the earthly, the lowly,
you find that you can concentrate now on the great questions of
the spiritual life. The incense swirls over your head and sweeps
you into itself. Why am I here? What am I meant to do here? How
can I do what my tiny little world needs with my equally tiny self?
Then you know what the incense is telling you in very physical
ways: The presence of God is patent, flagrant, manifest. You live
safely in the arms of God. There is work for you to do here. Then
you know that you were indeed right, even as a child: When the
incense came out in church, it was a serious time, a special time,
an important time, a consciousness-raising time, and God was
with you, as scripture says, "in the cloud."

But even without all the life data to back up its value to the
human nervous system, there are even greater gains to be had
from the burning of incense. It signals the time out of time. It
calls you to take a conscious time apart, to quiet the confusion
around you and within you. Incense invites you into another part
of life, the part that the pace of modern society tramples. You incense the Gospel book and remember the holiness you learned
from it. You incense the icons and the Eucharist and know that
you are in the presence of a greater dimension of life. You light the
Easter candle weekly and remember when you see the grains of

incense now embedded in it that the Christ-life still lies burning in your heart as you perfume the light.

Because of the incense you find yourself wrapped in a different one of your five senses: beyond hearing, beyond tasting, beyond seeing, beyond touching to the very center of yourself. As you breathe in its sweet odor of promise, of potential, of the power of the spirit, you find yourself between two worlds, one now and one to come. It brings you into union and unity with the rest of the universe.

Incense marks your very plebeian self and the spaces you inhabit as special space, as safe space. Even more than that, however, in its cloud you see yourself as part of the sacred space you too often take for granted, see only as humdrum, as commonplace, as routine.

Incense softens your experience of life. It makes pungent your experience of death, and it brings honor to every living thing as you incense the congregation itself as sacred, as holy. It is the monastic spirit that incense captures, yes, but it is the monastic heart that keeps the message of the incense alive: You and I are all part of the holy, all surrounded by the presence of God, all resting in the heart of God, and all called to do the will of God, whose work on earth is also our own. It is simply a matter of making that idea real, of wrapping yourself in the mist that is the mark of the universal spirit of life.

Incense marks our very plebeian selves and the spaces we inhabit as special space, as safe. Even more than that, however, in its cloud we see ourselves as part of the sacred space we too often take for granted, see only as humdrum, as commonplace, as routine.

35

MEMENTO MORI

On Valuing Yesterday

**The monastic memory of the dead is a long one. Entire books
have been written to preserve the names of Benedictine
monastics who were prominent in Europe over
the centuries. They go before us like light at midnight.**

In our own monastery, the necrology board—the record of deceased members of the Erie Benedictine community—archives the life and death of every sister who has entered this monastery from the time of our foundation in the United States in 1856. The three young women who came from Bavaria to work with the German immigrants of the region opened a house in Erie and are still very much alive to us.

Even more interesting, perhaps, is the fact that when I entered the monastery in 1952, the community was still reading a worn and dog-eared old book called *The Benedictine Martyrology*. Every day during table reading at noon, while the community ate in silence, we heard the names and short biographies of deceased Benedictines from all over Europe who had died even before the ninth century. They were the carriers of the Order, the saints of our beginnings, the ones who handed it all down to us.

That old book got lost when we moved the monastery from

town to countryside as antiques are wont to do at such times. But to this day, the names of every sister who entered this community and died here are read aloud on their death anniversaries. "Today let us remember," we pray, "Sister Gertrude Flynn, who died on this day in 1873." Visitors confess to being astounded to hear such a thing.

But why? As far as we're concerned those sisters founded us, built us, paid dearly to educate and prepare us to serve this world. They left a living and eternal model in their own lives of what it means not only to begin something but to see it through. To the end. Our Benedictine sisters and brothers don't leave us; they just stay with us differently. They move on before us to somewhere else for us to follow. In our hearts, their courage and sacrifices and glories still live. They left a path in Erie, Pennsylvania, over 160 years wide for us to remember, to learn from, to emulate, and to extend—as they did.

After fifteen hundred years of monasticism, tradition is a very Benedictine thing. It is not a trapdoor to the past, however. On the contrary. Our past prods us daily to go on, to do more, to be more. We stand on the shoulders of heroines, and they lived in an era when women were expected to be invisible to the public world.

Someday each of our own names will be inscribed on that board. Then a new generation will realize that every one of us made this monastery whatever it is. They will realize, as we do, how important we really are to one another and to the people we serve in this little area of the globe.

So when the local cemetery association told us that our graves were sinking and needed to be raised, we ordered new tombstones and brought all the old ones back to the monastery. There was a very important place for them here. They are used now to cover the pillars of the outdoor walkway that runs between the two wings of the monastery. As we pass the cloister garden that lies between them, we touch the tombstones, read the names of our ancestors, say a prayer for each, and not only remember again what we owe them for literally holding us up but also remember our own importance, like theirs, to do the same here and now.

Integrating the Practice

"Tradition," the liturgist Godfrey Diekmann, OSB, said, "is not the stuff we pass on. It is the passing on of the stuff." The "stuff"— the particulars of life—changes from generation to generation for everyone. First, for instance, our foundresses opened a boarding school. Twenty-five years later, they made it a nonresidential, four-year day school. What they passed on to us was not a prescribed form of education; it was a commitment to prepare young people to take their proper place in the development of this young country, however we needed to do it. In that we were one. Clearly, our tradition guides us, but it is not meant to ensnare us in yesterday. By remembering our dead, we find the strength to do things newly again.

When a sister dies, the monastery bell rings a solemn tone to call us to our last time together with her. It's then we understand what it means "to live on" in someone. The body goes to God. But the spirit remains here, is ours to preserve. It's the spirit of the sister that stays on. Death is always the launch of another phase of life for those who are left behind. And for us, too. The fact is that life is made of memories, not moments. The moments go; the memories stay forever. The change disorients us, of course, but the impact of our sisters' influence, the model of their indomitable commitment lives on in us. It stabilizes us, reminds us that we are part of the chain that keeps the message alive even as it dies a link at a time in front of our faces.

Just as a death in a family shatters a bit of our sense of ourselves, a death in the community reminds us of what we, too, must become to those who are now depending on us to show them the way. It reminds us of our obligation to teach them where we all came from and why. How we settled. To do what? What our dreams were then and how we worked them through. And most of all, what this death demands of us immediately.

Death is about extracting from each of the people in our lives what it is that makes life right. What is it that gives life meaning? What is it that, over the years, enabled us to become more than we were before we met one another? And now how will we maintain in our lives the very things we have just lost—a person of joy, respect, reverence, holiness, vision, whatever. Whatever the loss of this now deceased sister calls out in us we must maintain, so that our own lives may be full, even if our numbers have shrunk a bit.

The point is that the memories we leave of ourselves in others will someday determine our legacy for the future: Just as for our families it's Aunt Emily's smile, Uncle Lou's stories, Grandma's quiet presence. Or in our case Sister Maureen's vision, Sister Theophane's strength, Sister Mary David's openhearted approach to life. It's those things—the memories of those people—that we tuck away inside ourselves to get us through life when the days are dark and times are tragic and the resources are tight and the apparent differences between us are deep.

Every generation is the mirror and the energy of the one we've left behind. "The body dies," the Buddha's *Dhammapada* says, "but the Spirit is not entombed."

Tradition and its long line of living memories, in fact, is a lifeline. When there is no clear path before you, when you're on your own with no compass to lead you, then you realize how important it is to have someone behind you. It's to them that you can look for support, for a sense of possibility in periods that look as hopeless to you as theirs must have looked to them. It's not the past you seek. It is the model, the energy of the past that's important. As the poet-monk Basho puts it, "I do not seek to follow in the footsteps of the old. I seek the things they sought."

Our tradition guides us, but it is not meant to ensnare us in yesterday. By remembering our dead, we find the strength to do things newly again.

36

CANDLES

On Spiritual Illumination

**As liturgical symbols, candles bring a sense of connection be-
tween heaven and earth. In a monastery, the Easter candle or
Mass candles or processional candles become the focal points
of the liturgy, signaling the presence of God in our midst.**

After a woman makes perpetual profession of her monastic
vows of obedience, stability, and metanoia, she lights her
profession candle and carries her vow paper to the altar. In front
of the Prioress she signs the document that commits her to the
monastic way of life and leaves the candle still burning on the
altar. That same candle will be lit and taken to the altar again,
years later, at the times of her silver and golden jubilees. Finally,
after her death, the candle is set in its holder on a table in the
center of the chapel and lit during every part of the Divine Office
for thirty days.

The profession candle is the shimmering reminder that the
monastic vowed to follow the Light of Christ—the Jesus of the
Gospel—to the end. It marks, too, however, her soul becoming a
beacon for others to follow as they, too, go on trimming the wicks
of their own lives.

My profession/death candle sits in front of me daily as I write this book. It is the living memory of the light in my soul that brought me to this community, to this altar, to this life, to this moment. It is a reminder to me that its light and warmth must help others to find their own ways through life.

The question is: In what ways do candles contribute to the development of the spiritual life? How can I myself help that happen?

Candles, for all their fragility, are, in fact, the overwhelming images of what it means to be spiritually alive. In them is ancient energy, perpetual light, sign and symbol of possibility, of help on the horizon.

Does life smother us often? Yes, but the candle flares and reminds us to get up again and follow the Light of Christ—even when it seems we can't do it for one more minute, even as the flame weakens, even as the wax softens.

Does life leave us in darkness often? Yes. Which is exactly when the candle reminds us to raise the Light of Christ in ourselves. It's that light of hope and trust in us that we live to shine into the darkened lives of those whose own inner lights are weakening now. We live to light the candles of others in times of darkness so that none of us may collapse just when we need strength most.

Do we ourselves ever slip into darkness so severe that we cannot see our way out of it? Yes, and, at that point, the candle reminds us to believe that the light is with us, in us, showing us the way even when we cannot see a certain path.

Have we ever given in to darkness, to the feeling of failure, to the notion of impossibility, to a sense of light flickering weakly within? Of course. But it is just then that the lighted candle reminds us that, having been saved from our own weakness before, we will be strengthened by this community, by this Gospel, by this burning candle, which recalls to us the eternal presence of God, to the Jesus-path still in front of me. The candle itself becomes a steady, ever-steady, eternal presence and small light in each soul.

Light is clearly the oldest symbol in the Judeo-Christian tradition. The lighting of the Sabbath candles, long before the coming of Christianity, symbolized the presence of the God who is light. To the rabbis, the light of the candle was at the same time always new, always changing, and always the same. It was the ultimate symbol of the God who, in creating humankind out of the substance of goodness, was, nevertheless, not diminished. To Christians, light was a sign of new life in Jesus.

Like centuries of Jewish congregations before us, we stand to bless the Light. Like the moment of creation, the new week begins with a promise of life and growth and insight, and the presence of the God who is Light in the darkness and ongoing life in the spiral that is all our lives.

Integrating the Practice

The liturgical use of light in the Christian tradition, the reminder of the God who is Energy and Life, is a clear one in our monastery. Every Advent we watch together as each week another small candle points to the coming of the Light that is Christ. On Christmas Eve we bless the lighting of the Christmas tree, which is ever green and always a sign of eternal life. Every week of Lent we light another lantern in the chapel hall designed to lead us to the lighting of the new Easter flame.

Every night of our lives the monastery bell tower is flooded in light, a reminder of the Light that brings life and so makes our lifestyle of reflection and contemplation logical and necessary. At the same time, even in a technological age, we use candles to this day, the reminders that God is light, that we are part of the everlasting flame of life, that shadows everywhere are expelled by the tiniest pinpoints of light. If we will only light them.

Embedded in my soul is a story from the Islamic tradition. It has changed my life, my mental attitude toward darkness, toward difficulties, even toward what I have to understand is the obligation to dissent from darkness. The story tells of a Sufi, a member of one of Islam's monastic orders, who was found scratching through dust on the road and had quickly attracted a crowd of onlookers.

"Sufi, what are you doing?" the people asked.

"I lost my treasure and I'm searching for it," the Sufi answered.

So, one by one for hours and hours the people passing by dropped to their knees to sift through the dirt and dig in the ditches.

Finally, exhausted by the heat of the day and the fruitlessness of the task, a searcher sighed. "Sufi, are you sure you lost your treasure here?"

And the Sufi answered, "Oh, no, I didn't lose my treasure here. I lost it over there on the other side of the mountain."

The tired searchers were shocked. "If you know that you lost your treasure over there," they demanded, "why in the name of Allah are you searching for it here?"

And the Sufi said, "Because there's more light here."

You must forever ask yourself where you are looking for the treasure of life, where it is dark or where it is light. Where do you go for guidance through life? Does your own life give good light for others to steer by? In this great technological, complex, complicated, and divided world, you dare not take those answers for granted.

Candles, for all their fragility, are, in fact, the overwhelming images of what it means to be spiritually alive. In them is ancient energy, perpetual light, sign and symbol of possibility, of help on the horizon.

37

THE ABBOT/PRIORESS

On Leadership

Abbots and Prioresses are the spiritual leaders of female and
male Benedictine communities. They are chosen from
the community, by the community.

Authority in a monastic community is not gained by heredity
or imposed by force. Prioresses (Abbesses) and Abbots do
not succeed to these positions by inheritance, secular power, or
wealth. In fact, they are chosen by the community. Of all things
in that era, the democratic structure itself, with or without popular elections, was no small addition to humanity in the sixth century.

To this day the role of an Abbot or Prioress is to assure the
spiritual well-being of each autonomous monastic community, to
develop the monastery itself, and to see to the care of each and
every monastic. These leaders are the hubs, the centers, the
standard-bearers of life in the monasteries/abbeys. In them, we
seek models of our own search for God. To them we entrust the
integrity of the Rule and the spiritual energy and direction of the
community.

Perhaps the most unlikely thing to come out of sixth-century
Italy was, first, the Rule of Benedict itself—an entirely new type

of monastic life—and, second, the kind of leadership this new lifestyle called for in a period of political chaos, slavery, and authoritarian/hereditary control.

But what are we really talking about here? One of the common aphorisms applied to American society and culture, for instance, is an old one. It is also an incorrect one. "The business of America," President Calvin Coolidge is purported to have said in 1925, "is business." But the truth of the matter is that Coolidge really said, "The *chief* business of America is business." Not the only business or business to the exclusion of everything else.

The confusion between these two positions has marked the country for almost one hundred years. Are Americans about business only? Hardly. Monastics have one of those rhetorical confusions, too. They know that a single phrase misstated can affect the character of an institution for years. For instance, the interpretation of the statement "Monastics are to keep silence." Does this mean regularly? totally? always? That question divided communities for centuries. And just as there are other ways to look at the various elements of life, there are multiple ways to lead groups in pursuit of their values and goals. In the end, however, it's what we mean by leadership that will determine the kind of life we get.

In this instance, Benedict calls his community leaders Abbots, Abbesses, or Prioresses, familial terms of father and mother. Clearly, what they are to lead is not so much an organization as it is a way of life. A way to be in the world without feeling that I have lost my life to some anonymous corporation, to an assembly line, to a public I can't see, to a small room in a big building, to a work that was chosen for me to learn—whether I was drawn to it or not. Or worse, to a business over which I have no control. In the Rule we live like a family and are led as a family. The Prologue is clear: "Listen carefully, my daughter/son, to my instructions, and attend to them with the ear of your heart. This is advice from one who loves you; welcome it, and faithfully put it into practice."

One thing we know for sure: Whatever the rhetorical error in the repetition of Coolidge's comment that "the chief business of America is business," there is no doubt that American business concentrates on business first. In fact, workers owe their personal allegiance to the company, and the company owns whatever individual objects or intellectual properties its workers produce.

Even more to the point, businesses search over and over for new kinds of leadership, new strategies of leadership, new incentives for leadership, new tricks of leadership. They try various approaches to the reorganization of the work. They bring in new managers from every pool: pacesetters, autocrats, transformational leaders. They create bureaucratic division managers, they try democratic teamwork, they focus their workers on what is best for business. They do not emphasize or give preeminent concern to the possible effects of their business models on either the personal lives of their employees or their personal spiritual growth as they do their work. After all, it's the workers themselves who are expected to be loyal to the company; the company has no obligation whatsoever to their personal needs.

But this is not so in Benedictinism. Here leadership is for the sake of the monastics' personal growth. It's not a strategy designed to get more work out of people. It's not a lesson or a program. It's a life lived among brothers and sisters with a familial figure as guide and protector, wisdom figure and carrier of the good news of the Gospel—that we are all free, all bent on doing the same will of God, all committed to one another's best. Benedictinism is not only a "way of life"; it is a life on the way to the fullness of the Gospel, the community of life on the way to God.

Integrating the Practice

In an age and place of the total collapse of sixth-century Rome, monasticism takes a completely different approach to leadership. Benedict looks first and foremost at the Abbot and Prioress themselves. He wants community leaders who will hold up the standards of the Gospel as the mark of the community. He wants teachers who will instill "the leaven of divine justice." Where justice is not, neither is there a real monastery of equals, which, devoted to the Gospel, is the model of Jesus.

He wants the Prioress and Abbot in the first line of public models. He wants them to embody the vision, to be seen by the community "to hold the place of Christ." They themselves must do what they teach. They must truly lead so that the monastics can follow with confidence the sanctity of their vision. They must seek first the reign and justice of God. So if it is time to go to the streets to save the poor, the Abbot and the Prioress are expected to be in the front of the line. Or, at the very least, public voices of commitment to the needs of the poor, signs of the vision the community seeks. However distressed that might make the civic community.

Second, Benedict is clear, there must be no favoritism: Free men are not treated better than slaves. Instead he does the unthinkable: He opens monastic life to slaves themselves, who in the monastery are then free. What's more, he measures every person's influence in the community, both slave and free, by rank—by the date of their entry into the community and "by their humility and good works," not by their social status or their families' wealth or their good connections in society.

Most of all, he teaches, the leaders must care for the soul—for what's best for each monastic in the community. Abbots and Prioresses must be person-centered, not profit-centered. They must never use resources as an excuse for not doing what monastics must do to bring the reign of God to the people of God. If necessary, they are to correct the trend toward disregard of the world's needs and lead the community on to social justice with courage.

Until Daniel Goleman's book *Emotional Intelligence* came along to enable us to see that there is no such thing as intelligence but only multiple intelligences—various gifts, different perspectives on life, unique ways of dealing with life and its challenges, its problems—people were measured against one standard: one another. But in Benedictine monasteries, there remained the memory of another way of living life, of interacting with particular personalities, of making creativity, rather than conformity, the hallmark of the healthy community. Another way of relating, beyond either the manipulative or the forceful, still stirred, still ran through the Benedictine bloodstream.

In a Benedictine monastery, most people are measured by their gifts. The Abbot or Prioress is to deal with different personalities in the way that is best for each, with care, with compassion, with support. In fact, monastic leadership, the Rule teaches, is to accommodate and adapt to the various personalities and what is best for each. No authoritarianism here. No one size fits all. No take-it-or-leave-it obedience here. Just listening, listening, listening to the needs of the other.

Of all the approaches to leadership, the gentlest of all is reserved for those with whom the Abbot or Prioress is least able to connect on a personal level. There is no abandoning a person simply because they see differently than the others or, in fact, simply because they do not seem to see much at all. Instead, these differences give opportunities for discussion, for perpetual growth at every level and in every situation.

In order to convert, to cure the hurts, to change the path, to touch compassionately those who go unmoved by the call to become their best, most generous, most committed selves, the Rule teaches, the community leaders are to send *senpectae*—friends, wisdom figures, spiritual guides. The Abbot or Prioress is, in other words, to send "mature and wise" monastics—who have already negotiated every aspect of personal growth and so know its value—to console and comfort the struggling ones. These counselors are not to threaten. They are to urge those they are guiding to see the wisdom of what's needed and so comply with the community that cares for them. They are, Benedict says, "to confirm for the unhappy one the love of the community for them."

It is leadership for the led. It is leadership for those who truly want to grow. It is leadership for the good of the entire community. It is the kind of leadership—and institution—that has lasted for precisely that reason.

No, the chief business of the monastic community is not business. And, no, leadership is not practiced by force or gimmicks or economic rewards here. Leadership here is grounded in caring for the very soul, the heart, the upholding, the carrying, the leading, the loving of all. It is for the long, empty road of life to where it ends in the joy of the spirit at peace, in happiness, in community as together we grow deeper and deeper in the spirit of Jesus and the will of God.

Monastic leadership, the Rule teaches, is to accommodate and adapt to the various personalities and what is best for each. No authoritarianism here. No one size fits all. No take-it-or-leave-it obedience here. Just listening, listening, listening to the needs of the other.

38

CONTEMPLATION

On Seeing as God Sees

Contemplation is the practice of coming to see the presence
of God at the center of the natural world, in the midst of our
personal lives, as the light that emblazons our scriptures
and so leads us into even greater insight into God.

The rigors of orthodoxy and the depth of contemplation are
two very different things.

Orthodoxy brings us to accept the power and place of creed,
of tradition. By introducing us to the insights and practices of
those who have gone before us, it confirms in us the longtime
certainty that what we seek is findable and what we desire is doable and what we can become spiritually, as a result, is real, acces-
sible, life-giving. We know that because we have seen it in others.

Clearly, many across time have shown us that God-contact
comes through three levels: sacred reading, natural experience,
and the conscious awareness of God in the experiences of life.

We come to understand what it was in our early formation
that guided us through the commonplaces of time to a consciousness of the Life beyond life. Ancient practices, regular prayer
forms, feasts, and feria days marked the flow of life and gave us
the patterns of spiritual regularity and goodness that could launch

us into the spirit of the otherworldly that has so long launched others beyond the exercises of religion into the realms of the truly spiritual. Those are the things that tell us what we are to think about religion and what we need to do to live it well.

Contemplation is different. In contemplation we wrestle with the meaning behind all those words and practices. We begin to realize the presence of God in life. In our own lives. We become more concentrated on knowing the mind of God rather than limiting the spiritual life to the traditional use of religious things—candles and incense, chant and prayer forms—as magnetic and enriching as they are. Instead, we begin to see the face and heart of God everywhere, in different kinds of people, even in different ways of talking about God. Contemplation replaces the law of God with the love of God. We cease to think so much about the fear of hell and concern ourselves with the real meaning of fidelity to the mind of God.

Contemplation is not the practice of saying prayers. It is the growing, overwhelming consciousness of God within us and around us, before us and beyond us. It is God embedded in our souls and at the helms of our hearts. It is the awareness of God that is, as Paul says, "pray[ing] without ceasing."

What we have come to know about God we now begin to live in our daily lives: that Black lives matter, for instance; that women are equal to men and as much bearers of the Spirit as men will ever be; that everything we do as individuals, as countries, must reflect the will of God for all of creation. Suddenly we realize that God is everywhere, is alive in our lives, is the light on the road that beckons us on.

Every major religious tradition calls us beyond forms of religion to faith in God, to depth of soul. Then, when the soul is as broad as the sky, we are ready to break down the false boundaries between peoples. We are spiritually mature enough to center ourselves on the fulfillment of the God-life within us rather than simply make the things of God our gods. Now we are able to focus more on the presence of God rather than make keeping the Latin Mass our highest spiritual purpose. We're able to find that arguing about old prayer translations is less important than reconsidering the possibility of girl servers at Mass. We become aware that the way the Church distributes communion is less important than the way we interpret the "inerrancy" of scripture and so the place of personal reflection in our spiritual direction.

The deification of things is everywhere in religion. Through this a false orthodoxy—meaning keeping things the way they've "always been"—becomes the goal and the will of God for creation becomes less of the essence of our spirituality and more like a distraction on the way.

Islam puts it this way: Once upon a time a Sufi made the annual pilgrimage to Mecca. It was a long walk for him, and the sun was high. He had come miles without stopping. Finally, in sight of the great mosque at Mecca, sure of the goal now, the old man lay down in the road to rest.

Suddenly one of the other pilgrims shook him awake, rough and harsh in the doing of it. "Wake up," he commanded. "You blaspheme, Sufi! You lie in such a way that your feet are pointed toward the holy mosque! What kind of Sufi are you?"

The old Sufi opened one eye, smiled a bit, and said, "I thank you, holy sir. Now would you be kind enough to turn my feet in some direction where they are not pointed toward God."

There is a difference between prayer and contemplation. Prayer says the words. Contemplation understands that in the end the right words don't really matter. In contemplation we discover that there is a difference between orthodoxy and the consciousness of God in life.

So often rule keepers remember to keep the rules because rule keeping is so safe. All I have to do to be holy, I assume, is to check off the practice, while I forget, if I ever knew, its purpose in life. Contemplation, on the other hand, goes beyond the spine or structures of a religious community, beyond its customs books or rule books or historical development to its innards, to its mystical end, to the energy that created it and drives it. The contemplative life is more than Christian prayers or rituals or sermons. It is all of those things but more. It is about the experience of God on the individual level. It is the fullness of the Tradition come to life again in us as the personal sensibility of what it is to realize that it is in the womb of God that we live and breathe and have our being.

Integrating the Practice

Contemplation is the lived experience of knowing, really knowing, that God is around you, beyond you, behind you, calling you, moving you, urging you within your deepest self to find the more of Life here and now.

Great Christian contemplatives—along with contemplatives from every great spiritual tradition—Rumi, the Sufi poet; Dogen, the Japanese Zen master; Thich Nhat Hanh, the Buddhist sage; Vivekinanda, the Hindu ascetic—are signs to you of the spiritual peace that comes when you immerse yourself more and more in the presence of God in your own life rather than simply in the rote exercises of religion for their own sake. Then nature becomes a springboard to the awe of God. Scriptures become your testimony to the will of God for the world. Your own life becomes proof that God has already been with you every step of the way. It is only a matter now of engaging in the dialogue of the heart, where the Spirit of God waits for you to open your mind and heart to let God in. You come to realize, thanks to the witness of all those contemplatives who have gone before you, that contemplation is not a special gift, an unusual gift, a preternatural gift. It is part of what it means to be a fully developed spiritual human being, and it allows you to perceive life from a greater depth of soul than you were aware you had.

Contemplation is not a spiritual "practice" in the normal sense of the word. It is the end product of all those spiritual practices that have led you to the heart of God and the awareness of God in your heart, in your mind, in your life choices, wrapped round in an aura of God-consciousness that is beyond any need for words or for spiritual exercises. It is the end result of endless consciousness that God is, indeed, truly "with us." Then, the spiritual life becomes a link between your own outer and inner selves. Then you experience human life as proof that there are greater experiences of life to come.

True contemplation is the wholesome, sane, happy, joyful, and openhearted sign of those who walk naturally with God and live with the purpose of bringing the will of God to life, who are truly contemplative.

Contemplation is not the practice of saying prayers. It is the growing, overwhelming consciousness of God within us and around us, before us and beyond us. It is God embedded in our souls and at the helms of our hearts.

39

~

HUMILITY AND
THE PRESENCE OF GOD

On the Presence of God

**Humility is the oxymoron of the spiritual life. It leads us to
personal development, not to humiliation. The monastic life
is built on twelve steps of a spiritual ladder, each of them
another degree toward a holy, happy life.**

Acceptance of the presence of God in life is the beginning of a
real spiritual life rather than simply the exercise of pious
practices. Acceptance of our own emptiness—the awareness that
God is God and we are not—turns us inside out and upside down
until we meet God where God really is—in us. Then we find God
where we are, the God who made us, who companions us through
life, who calls us like a magnet to the best of ourselves all our days.
It is when we recognize the presence of God in our lives that life
takes on a holy hue. The very moment we unveil our nothingness
and find it full of God rather than full of ourselves the spiritual
life really begins.

At the center of Benedict's treatise on the monastic life and
spirituality is a very disarming chapter on humility. It is the longest chapter in the tiny Rule. It is the core of Benedict's concern

for human development, the cornerstone—the heart—of Benedictine spirituality. It is a template for spiritual fulfillment and
human development.

Interestingly enough, it is not about the need for great asceticism, determined withdrawal from the world, or the terms of personal perfection required in a spiritually spartan world. It's about
our journey through life. It's about the way we go about being
human. It's about who we are in the human community. It is
about our relationship with God.

And that's where the first surprise lies. In the first four steps of
humility, Benedict makes statements that transform our understanding of spirituality. The first step of humility, Benedict teaches,
"is to keep God before our eyes at all times." Most programs that
purport to guide us along the path of holiness to the arms of God,
promise to show us how to find God. God, they say, is the end
and the goal of the perfect life. If we do this . . . we will earn God,
we're taught; if we do that . . . we will find God. If we are perfect
we will attain union with God. Really? Instead Benedict is telling
us that we don't have to "find" God because we already have
God—in us, around us, before us, guiding us through life.

Recognizing the difference between various kinds of "merit
theology" and Benedict's spiritual cosmography is the first step.
The singular truth, Benedict teaches, is this: God is in the center
of our very being, in the manifestation of creation, in every breath
we take. The question, then, is not whether God is with us in life;
the question is Are we with God, who is waiting for us to realize
this relationship?

For those for whom God is present, God is there. For those for
whom God is not present, God is still there, but they are not. It is
from that consciousness of God in our lives that the three other
dimensions of our relationship spring.

The second step of humility is to realize that, if God is with us always, then no matter what happens to us, no matter how difficult life may seem, in the end God's will—not ours and our attempts to control life—will be best for us. No, God does not will us lung cancer as some kind of ghoulish test. It is the natural interplay of chemistry and biology that does that—but God, Benedict teaches us, will be with us as we struggle through it, holding us up, urging us on, and accompanying us spiritually and emotionally as we grow.

The third step is to attend to this relationship with God, because it needs careful development, needs guidance to help us chart our ways, to keep us spiritually centered on the dark days. Benedict sees the Abbot or Prioress as the spiritual guide of every monastic. And that is certainly true at one level. At the same time, the figures we ourselves choose as spiritual directors and guides through life will have a great deal to do with how we respond to our circumstances, how we strengthen our relationships to God— as a martinet or a lover? Having someone in this role in our lives is very important for us all, or trying to be our own guides and spiritual directors may well leave us with nothing but a bad case of the blind leading the blind.

The danger points in life—times of deep depression or overwhelming disappointment—are times of great change or great challenge. It's then that we most need a sounding board, someone who can hear us wander up and down the darkling tunnels of life with no sure path to follow and call us back to rethink it all again. We need those who will help us test the byways of our lives on criteria of character as well as success, of happiness as well as excitement, of holiness as well as religion. Most of all, we need to present the truth of ourselves to wisdom figures who can help us see ourselves as we are.

Then, in this grappling with the search for our true selves, we must persist. It is humility—the ability to trust the presence of

God, to be honest in our pursuit of the petulant desires that are driving us, to seek spiritual guidance in our attempts to grow beyond whatever it is that is blocking us from becoming our best selves. It's then and then only that we can come to wholeness, to the awareness that God is with us on the Way. Then, life in all its complexities becomes simple, becomes truly open to the call of God to become our real selves—with all that implies of integrity, of authenticity, and of openness to the goodness of life, and without the burdens that come from pretending to be what we are not.

The fourth degree is to understand that we need a confidant, someone with whom we are starkly honest. Someone who is honest, is true, has character. It's so easy to fall into the trap of impressing people. To start to grow, we need to own our mistakes, our wild dreams and childish certainties, our attempts to hide our weaknesses or our dangerous forays into groundless fantasies about the spiritual life.

Integrating the Practice

Perhaps the most compelling truth of life, the one that makes you rethink everything you think you know about God and personal growth and the secret of life, is simply this: God is with you now, and here, and always. You don't have to get God, to earn God. You have God already and always will.

Coming to an understanding of your place in creation, in life, and in the human enterprise determines the quality of your life. Humility, the genuine, rock-bottom awareness that you are neither more nor less good, right, knowing, holy, than any other human being around you, becomes the gold standard of spiritual maturity. Humility is the metric by which you may evaluate the credibility of the truly spiritual person. Anything else is pure religious posturing.

You want—you expect—success as it is measured in a two-car-garage world. You plan to live on tree-lined avenues. You expect to work in skyscrapers. You want to own a boat and a summer house. That's success. You want it all.

At one level, there's nothing wrong with any of that. Except for this: It stands to take from you exactly what you think it will bring. A sense of security wanes with the compulsion to get more and more and more. The "moreness" of material things is camouflage for the real thing.

Despite the fact that no one can live in more than one house, sail in more than one boat, drive more than one car at a time, you too often surrender your life to the dreams of getting them. Instead, Benedict's treatise on humility tells you that there is another, simpler, happier way to go through life. The Rule of Benedict says that, actually, you do have it all! You have a good life, meaning a life based on a sense of enoughness, and a good God, who has provided the best for you if you will only train your appetites to the real and the lasting. That, Benedict says, is the best life a person can get. It is the notion, the awareness, the experience of the presence of God that wraps you round. It carries you through life, it touches you in everything you do, it waits for you to live in that presence, consciously, with the certainty that comes from faith.

God is with us now, and here, and always. We don't have to get God, to earn God. We have God already and always will.

40

HUMILITY AND THE ESSENCE OF THE SELF

On the True Self

To be totally happy and wholly developed, our interior selves
and our exterior self must be the same person. It is the
work of a lifetime to become my true self.

In steps five through eight of his ladder of humility, Benedict
turns the inner light of the Rule squarely on the spiritual camouflage of the personal life as the impasse to happiness. He begins
the simple but specific role of peeling away the layers of the self in
order to navigate the real road to holiness and the development of
the true self.

The fact is that images and imaginings are the cloth out of
which modern people are cut. There are patterns already fresh and
established out there to choose from: Just as the childhood rhyme
says, "Butcher, baker, candlestick maker"—bankers, financiers,
business owners; they are reality-show characters all. But they are
at the same time profiles already highly sought after as marks of
success, security, and social aplomb in a world built on paper
money and ready-made commercial résumés.

We have been following the templates for so long that the real miracle of life is that anybody actually knows who they are anymore—and admits it. Instead, the images come early and often. Television, magazine covers, film stars, Madison Avenue posters capture the screens of our lives, show us how to dress, where to work, how to talk and walk, and what to pursue in life. Eventually, our true selves are papered over, too. Then finding our way back to ourselves, past our fears and our failures, is so long gone we hardly know ourselves, let alone let anyone else know us. The result, of course, is lives powered by other people's scripts. We become a population of wannabes. And our lives are filled with a sense of failure or fundamental distrust, even of ourselves. We can't tell others who we are or what we've done or what we'd like to do or what we can't pretend any longer. We live in a perpetual state of hiding.

Then the Rule of Benedict exposes us to ourselves so that someday, if we will, we can start all over. We can begin again. We can discover what we ourselves really want to do instead of what families or friends or society think we should do. Step five of Benedict's ladder of humility begins to enable us to uncover ourselves. "We do not conceal any sinful thoughts entering our hearts," he says, "or any wrongs committed in secret." Unedited honesty is the first step in refusing to be two people: the one inside, which no one knows, and the one outside, which everyone is in awe of. Whether we deserve it or not.

At degree five, personal honesty is our best protector. After all, what can anyone do to harm us if we ourselves confess the struggles of our souls? It's not Bill Clinton's "I didn't inhale and never tried it again." It's Barack Obama's straightforward "Yes, I tried drugs when I was in college. Once. Never again."

At degree six, we make no demands on the universe, we harbor no false expectations. The Rule says that humble people "are content with the lowest and most menial treatment." We see ourselves as the beginners of life, learners—not masters of anything. Most of all, we do not exaggerate our own abilities or positions or value. We even stop expecting special treatment—like that table I can get at a great restaurant because everyone knows me, tickets to the show at the last minute, appointments with specialists the minute I call. We have learned by now that enough is enough—which means that we will never again be disappointed because we don't have the best, the biggest, the most sought-after brand of anything. We have a life that is just like everybody else's. And most important of all, we have finally become enough for ourselves. There is no need now to pretend, to posture about anything. We are finally free.

The seventh degree of the ladder is the most challenging of all. At this level, the Rule says we begin to realize that we are inferior—in some way—to everyone. There is nothing in the worst of people that is not also in me. Expressed or not, it's there. I have no room, no reason to crow about anything.

At that point, I have begun to taste the bread of humility: No one has anything I want; everyone has something I don't have, and that is perfectly all right. And yes, but for the grace of God, there go I. I am open, honest, stripped to the heart in front of the world and able to accept myself without having to tear others down so that I can raise myself up. This is a state of complete self-acceptance. It is the great moment of interior freedom: I have nothing to fear from anybody. No one can possibly expose my weaknesses because I myself have already done that.

Then the eighth degree of Benedict's ladder of humility ends on a quiet note. I won't show off again. I will live like everybody else, within the norms of the human community, and do

everything I can to maintain its goodness, its traditions, its holiness.

Integrating the Practice

The truly humble person understands how difficult it may have
been to learn these lessons but knows, too, that only when these
four steps have been climbed is one's soul really free. Free from
pretense, free from fear that others will see me as I really am, free
from social climbing and expectations of special treatment. Free
from the veils of superiority that lead to prejudice and papier-
mâché claims to proficiency. Free to really be myself—and be val-
ued for that alone.

Suddenly it all gets clear: Humility does not degrade you. Humility does not make you small. It makes you great. It means that
you can rejoice in everyone else's gifts and dreams. You can shine
on everybody else's masterpieces and you can be happy to be part
of their celebrations.

Humility means, as well, that you can rejoice in your own
abilities and joys but cling to none of them. Now nothing binds
you to your work or your status or your appearance. If those
things disappear you will still be yourself and loved for that reason
alone. If the mansion you spent your life building burns down,
you can be happy in a cabin on the land because nothing will
really have changed: You will always be yourself, no more, no less.
You have nothing to hide. You have no thing that is the definition
of your importance or your impact on the world.

You will be enough for you. You won't need to preen and am-
plify yourself. You won't need uniforms and diamonds to an-
nounce your value. You won't need power and posturing to
establish your credentials. Indeed, you will be enough for you—
and that is everything you need.

Humble people make no demands on the universe. They harbor no false expectations. The Rule says that humble people
"are content with the lowest and most menial treatment." We
see ourselves as the beginners of life, learners—not masters of
anything. Most of all, we do not exaggerate our own abilities
or positions or value.

41

HUMILITY AND THE MAKING OF COMMUNITY

On Building Community

Humility teaches us that we are here to join with
the rest of the human race in finishing the work that God
began but left to us to complete. To do that we have
to build the human community.

In his treatment of the spiritual life, Benedict earns the title he's
been given over the ages as "the Great Psychologist." Right. The
psychologist of the sixth century. He understood the human condition. He understood motivation and relationships. He understood depression and loneliness. He understood our illusions of
grandeur and our collapse under failure. Out of all that, he created another kind of lifestyle, another kind of obedience, another
kind of human community in a cauldron of classism, slavery, and
social deterioration.

While the powers that be in autocratic Rome ruled from
thrones of gold carried on the backs of underlings and slaves,
Benedict's vision of the world upended life as the socialites had
planned it for themselves. Benedict's world would emerge from
the heart of God, would thrive on the will of God, and would

become a world of equals in harmony with the universe and one another.

Benedict's view of the spiritual life began with the awareness of the presence of God rather than a lifelong jousting for God as a prize to be won—to be merited—by practicing so many religious devotions. Instead, he saw the ladder to heaven topped not by "winning God," but by human beings treating one another as human beings. That very schema of life—the presence of God, the conversion of the self, and the qualities of Christian community—upset the popular cosmology of slaves on the bottom of a ladder grasping for the God they cannot reach. Benedict's ladder of humility simply turns the vision of the spiritual life upside down and inside out. Steps nine, ten, eleven, and twelve on the ladder of humility deal with a world where humans are in harmony with one another and God is the ground of it all.

On the ninth step of the ladder, we are told to control our tongues. What weapon is more dangerous to any community than the speech that destroys some and suppresses others, creates emperors but enslaves innocent human beings in a captivity of derision? To keep silent in the face of division, to refuse to take sides, to resist carrying tales or spreading insult is a defense more powerful than the sword. What we do not say we cannot possibly be judged for, accused of, wounded by.

Keeping silent in the face of sin is its own evil, yes. Nevertheless, to stay silent for the sake of those who want mindless support for their personal power is the only antidote to partisanship and enmity. It is so easy to become a courtier of the powerful. But it will be impossible if we refuse to be part of the insidious social warfare it spawns.

The tenth step of the ladder of humility tells us not to be given to "ready laughter" and that "only fools raise their voices in laughter." When you read a sentence like this fifteen centuries after it was written, it's important to remember that laughter was seen as a problem everywhere until the fourteenth century. Philosophers and religious figures had decided that laughter broke the connection between reason and reality. Therefore, laughter was largely forbidden as gross and rude. What is being asked for here then is rationality: Think things through. Reflect. Be careful. Don't leap without listening. Don't be a fool.

Only Thomas Aquinas in the thirteenth century and Marsilio Ficino in the fifteenth decided that laughter was actually good for the soul. So as the centuries went by new interpretations had to be made. But in this original passage, the meaning is clear: Be sensible. Don't be crude or superficial about life. You are here for a serious purpose and you must be serious about it. Actually, that's good advice whatever the century. Laughter or no laughter.

The eleventh step of the ladder of humility asks us to speak "gently . . . seriously . . . briefly and reasonably, but without raising our voices." It's a holy act to enjoy life and to make it enjoyable for others. It is not holy to take up all the air in the room. It is not community building to dominate the thinking and voices of others. It is not an act of community to foment argument rather than engage in thoughtful discussion. To demand attention, to smother the ideas of others, to take away a group's need to be patient is not an act of community. It's civil war.

The twelfth step of the ladder of humility is the capstone of the spiritual life. This step is that "we always manifest humility in our bearing no less than in our hearts so that it is evident"—everywhere.

This step is clear: no bullying, no ridicule, no demeaning, no excluding, no suppressing. And most of all, no arrogance, no swishing through life demanding attention, no hysteria to get it.

Integrating the Practice

It is humility—your respect for others as well as your awareness of
your own limitations—that determines your regard in society,
your connections with the people around you. More than that,
humility is the measure of your spiritual authenticity. It's so easy
to pretend to be what you are not; it is so refreshing to simply be
yourself.

Clearly, the way you use your voice has a great deal to do with
whether or not humility mellows you in the development of society. The addendum is clear: Be quiet, be serious, be reasonable, be
humble enough to hear the ideas and concerns of everyone so that
the sense of community may grow and the needs of all are honored.

Humility, Benedict's ladder of spirituality, is a ready antidote
to racism, for instance. If only we were wise enough to grasp it.
Instead, we rank ourselves as the norm of humanity. But life is not
a matter of "we and they." It is a matter of them and us, all of us
being human together.

Only serenity can come from such things. First, the awareness
of God in you, forever, always gives you all the security you need.
You don't have to make up your own importance anymore. Second, the self-criticism that comes from self-knowledge levels life
to the point of self-acceptance. Now you can simply join the
human race, no better, no worse than the rest of humankind.
Most of all, you don't see yourself as superior to any of the rest of
us. We are all just in life together, meant to take care of one another, always intent on inclusion, on equality, on being sisters and
brothers looking out for one another. Then humility has done its
job. Then the world is safe for us all. And we're serene. Just what
the twelve degrees of humility foster. Just what monasticism offers.

No doubt about it, humility teaches you that you are not here on earth in order to control it or reject it, to avoid it or ignore it, to use it for your ends alone or to enslave the rest of the world to your designs. You and I are here to join the human race in finishing the work that God began but left to us to complete. To do that we have to build the human community. To be thoughtful, to include all the voices in the pursuit of truth and good, makes community *community*, a powerful voice in the middle of a fractured world.

It is not community building to dominate the thinking and voices of others. It is not an act of community to foment argument rather than thoughtful discussion. To demand attention, to smother the ideas of others, to take away a group's need to be patient is not an act of community. It's civil war.

42

THE MONASTIC

On "One Thing Only"

Monastics are monks and nuns who spend their lives in monasteries under one of the ancient monastic Rules that have formed religious life and society for over fifteen hundred years. They devote their lives to the one thing necessary— the search for God in life.

The questions are important ones: What is a monastic? What do monastics do? And how do they do it?

It's 5:30 A.M. There is no noise on the street yet. This hour, the early morning hour of Lauds, for morning praise, it seems, has been reserved for monastics alone, fresh with praise and gratitude, to start the day for the rest of the world. It is time to renew our trust in the presence of God among us. It is the moment to refresh our faith in the certainty that life has purpose, has meaning, has a sense of the Creator and a taste of creation that must shape our lives, that can be abandoned only at our peril. Indeed, monastic life is a sign of the eternal, a resting place on the Way, a breath of incense, a path lit by lights that lead to heaven. It takes a lifetime to mold a monastic heart in a society more concerned with the stock market, the election, the promotion, the security of it all.

The breeze behind the curtain, a soft and mild one, is wafting

across the old part of the city and down the lake road to our Benedictine monastery seven miles away. We have been on this in-
town property since our forebears arrived from Germany. We've
watched one generation of immigrants after another begin here in
the inner city and then move on to the small ethnic communities
that had formed around us. All of them different; all of them the
same. Every new group came looking for the same fresh start in
life, the same new opportunities, the same kind of support as they
adjusted to a strange society, a plethora of languages, an entirely
new government structure, and the social expectations and social
values that went with them.

In this neighborhood, the Germans came first, and we followed them. St. Walburga, the Benedictine Abbey of nuns, which
had been founded in Bavaria in 1035, sent us here in 1852 to
minister to German immigrants as they struggled to make the
transition from Europe to the United States. As immigrants, they
needed to learn the language, they needed education, they needed
spiritual support. If they were going to be able to find a faith community, as well as stepping-stones to the larger community, they
needed this tightly knit little international hamlet—with their
churches, their religious, their German Benedictine monastery in
the midst of them.

The Benedictine monks, also from Bavaria, built a church in
1857 and made the people a parish. Between the Benedictine
monks and the nuns, who came to this small area in 1856, strangers became home to one another. They were not alone any longer.
And neither were we. We were simply doing what monastics had
been doing for almost fifteen hundred years: creating community.
America, the polyglot of countries and inner-city communities
like our own, saw them all. First, the Irish, then the Polish, the
Blacks, the Russians, the Vietnamese, the Latinos, the Nigerians,
the Cubans, and now the Muslims and Bhutanese.

This is the public story of every monastery in the country. By the time of this writing, at least five hundred women have entered this monastery over the years to make it a home, a center, a place of welcome, and a spiritual light to some of the neediest immigrants in some of the darkest hours a people can have. Benedictine monastics anchored Europe after the fall of the Roman Empire and the loss of its government, the disappearance of its legions and the order they brought. We fed and housed, educated and employed, were available to and companions of those whose lives had no other support. We loved and launched every immigrant family and child within our reach.

Clearly, monasticism is not about a flight from life. On the contrary. The monastic life is a life in love with life. The difference between monasticism and any good organization is that we give our lives to being the light of the soul for many.

Integrating the Practice

Monastics live immersed in the scriptures, looking for the guidance to know what to do for people under stress. We make ourselves a model of the hope that strangers really can live together in peace. We call ourselves to bridge the differences between people. To become signs of what it means to live a holy, happy, and purposeful life together. We spend our lives immersed in the scriptures so that we can know when as a people, as human beings together, we are beginning to lose our way, to follow false prophets, to forget the ways of Jesus. We try to understand how the basics of the spiritual life and the needs of the people around us might become disconnected. Then from decade to decade we reach out to freshen those relationships again and again.

Our spiritual life, as God says to the prophets of Israel, is to warn the people of their departure from the Way. We are to be heralds in the camp who hear the Word of God and repeat it so that others may also find and keep the path. We are celibates who live a life of reflection on the Word of God. We ask the questions others either miss or cannot deal with when their own lives—their jobs, their children's education, their families' lives—depend on them.

It is one thing for us to denounce nuclear weapons, to protest gun legislation, to demand equality, to shout out loud against sexism, racism, inequality, and to be devoted to the fact that Black Lives Really Matter! But when a family is barely making it, when they need to work in industries that contribute to sexist, racist, militaristic culture—they cannot be expected to protest so much that they lose their own jobs. Then it is monastics who are free of that kind of public engagement that have the right, the obligation, to confront those issues, as monastics did for centuries before us. We live to establish communities of peace and justice. We live simple lives—as signs of what is possible in a culture which, instead, makes things and power the measure of success. Monastics live lives whose value is not computed by the plethora of things we own or by what we do not have. We set out to live ordinary, commonplace lives so that others may see life's superfluities and understand that losing them is no loss at all.

We divide our lives into times of choral prayer, private reflection and contemplation, useful service, personal development for the sake of others, and community building. In that way the hospitality and spiritual companionship we offer to others is as true of our lives together as is our care for theirs. We live full lives. We attend every day to the things of the soul, the spirit, the self, and the society around us. We live to be authentic voices of the love of God for us all. It is a template you can follow for a balanced and a happy life.

Our lives, our goods, our time, our care all belong to the people. We offer them words of faith, signs of love, an experience of home. And together we listen to the words of contradiction loud enough to signal all of us that we are living in a society that numbs us into becoming less than we are humanely meant to be.

To us there is only one thing that is important—and that is to live in the Presence of God for the things of God so that others may truly live also.

The monastic life in this particular monastery, like your own life, has had its challenges, its difficult decisions, its hard times to live through. But with it all, the breeze in the window at 5:30 A.M., cool and low, tells us that this life in the midst of toil and tumult is, nevertheless, a stable and steadfast one. It is a quiet life, a regular life, an intense life. This life, for both you and me, is about personal growth, communal growth, and human growth, all of them measured by the spiritual peace, growth, and light they give to everyone whose life we touch.

To us there is only one thing that is important—and that is to live in the Presence of God for the things of God so that others may truly live also.

43

STEWARDSHIP

On the Conservancy of Creation

Benedictine life is a life of stewardship, of caretaking. It's about having what is necessary to sustain ourselves with decency and dignity—as all people deserve. But it is not dedicated to the amassing of goods.

One of the great Benedictine virtues is "enoughness." The interesting thing about enoughness is that it is not imbued in the monastic by a chart or canon of weights and measures, as in "You may have three pair of shoes, one kind of soap, one visit home." No, the measurement Benedict specifies in the Rule is very straightforward, very obvious. Let the monastic have what she needs, the Rule teaches, and "those who have need of less, thank God."

Greed, we sense in this passage, is more a temptation than we ever knew. After all, if you can afford a thing, why not get it? Answer: Because every element we take out of the Earth is affecting the future of the earth, of our families, of world peace. To squander life on the amassing of goods simply for the sake of amassing goods only shrinks the soul to the size of the last pointless and superfluous item.

The problem is that a commitment to stewardship makes

every request a decision: Do I really *need* this thing, or do I simply *want* it? It confronts us with the difference between the cultural question Don't I deserve to keep up with the technology, the style, the convenience? and the moral question of what is being destroyed, denied to someone else if I join this pandemic of things. What is accumulation without cause doing to the breadth and quality of my own soul? This is surely the question of the age. But how many of us really realize that yet?

In sixth-century Europe—ablaze with petty wars and dispossessed peasants roaming the countryside looking for the basics of life—the Benedictine response was to drain and till bad land, to clear the fields and drain the swamps, to train and hire peasants to farm, until they seeded enough land to feed Europe. Monastics carry a legacy of ancestors who, across centuries, dedicated their lives to reclaiming the land and cultivating it for fruitfulness, for public nourishment, in an effort to steward their portion of the world well. They leave us a model for our own time. They cared for their land as if it were the Garden of Eden.

I remember as if it were yesterday taking some visitors through our monastery. The woman said to me, "My dear, the antiques are exquisite." I looked from item to item in the great parlor by the monastery doors. "Antiques?" I said, "What antiques . . . and where? These aren't antiques. They have been used in this monastery for a hundred and fifty years."

If I truly get only the things I need, everything I have doubles in value. If I can't take for granted that I will be able to get another one like it, everything I have becomes precious. Nothing can be taken for granted. I have to learn how to keep it, how to care for it, how to find the best use for it. Or when we find ourselves with multiple versions of the same thing, we have to figure out how to put what we don't need to use in important ways. Like how to move furniture to families in need rather than simply store and dust them daily.

Suddenly stewardship is at least as important as the vow of poverty, or surely as serious as refusing to get caught up in an ongoing, wild competition to have the latest, the best, the biggest assets, just in case. Then the humility the Rule extols takes over. Benedictinism becomes a clear gift of the Spirit as the sixth step of humility requires "to be content with the least, and most menial of treatment" rather than concentrated on financial security or personal convenience.

Integrating the Practice

The real value of stewardship lies in its equal concern and care for the past, the present, and the future. A life lived through the filter of stewardship saves things rather than discards them simply because they're old. If nothing else, you see that those who also need what you are getting rid of get it.

You begin to see that stewardship addresses life everywhere. Rather than simply abandoning your last computer for this new one means that you must find a use for it somehow. Stewardship is meant to buttress the weak ends of society so that all good things are available to all at some level of value. Or to put it another way, why are so many fancy old baby cribs, hung heavy with all the mobiles a child could ever need for mental stimulation, still sitting in garages when they should be in the homes of young couples who have no money to buy their own cribs? Or more important than that, perhaps, why are so many computers not given to young students whose parents can't possibly buy them?

Stewardship is a long-lost value in a society that equates success with newness. But there is another kind of problem as well.

With the invention of plastic, the value of stewardship got dealt a heavy blow. The explosion of plastic as a basic material brought too much debris to oceans that cannot be cleaned up, as were landfills before them. More than that, artisanship suffered. Too much good art got reduced to look-alikes. The world got too much faux this and faux that to learn the difference between simulation and the real thing. Authenticity became a value of the past.

Stewardship, then, brings up the question of preservation, of insisting on biodegradable, well-made real objects rather than the impermeable look-alikes that will kill off the fish, poison the land, while we never even have the grace to blush.

Preservation, conservation, authenticity, and moral impact mark the monastic charism of stewardship. This charism takes the world as it is and sets out to make it better. It gives itself to completing and protecting the work of creation. As the Rule says, "Then are they truly monks when they live by the work of their hands as did our ancestors before us."

One of the glories of Benedictine history is the number of centuries our ancestors dedicated their lives to reclaiming the land, in an effort to steward their portion of the world well. They leave us a model for our own time. They cared for their land as if it were the Garden of Eden.

44

THE DESERT

On Difficult Times

**The desert has been an icon of withdrawal and asceticism for
monks and nuns of Egypt and Syria since A.D. 270.
But no longer.**

After the legalization of Christianity by Constantine and its
concurrent designation by Theodosius as the state religion of
the Roman Empire, two kinds of Christians emerged. The first
group were the Christians of the catacombs, all of them early con-
verts to the faith, who had lived in the age of persecutions and
suffered the age of martyrdoms. The second group were those who
had simply been named Christian as part of their integration into
Rome's civil identity. As far as lifelong Christians who had suffered persecution, and even death, were concerned, simply nam-
ing people "Christian" did not really make them Christians. Not
down deep. Not in the bloodstream. Not for no effort, no risk at
all. Not for the price which the older generation of martyrs and
they themselves had paid. These two streams of Christianity—
political Christians and spiritually committed Christians—
seemed miles apart.

And yet, in the third century, another strain of the Christian
community had begun to form in the deserts around Egypt and

Syria under the guidance of Anthony the Great. With the period of martyrdom over, the question was how to simulate the same kind of meaningful sacrifice that had marked the commitment of the early Christians. The answer to the question was already waiting in the rise of these alternative desert communities.

Hermits, ascetics, and small Christian groups went out to the desert to find solitude for contemplation and to live lives of poverty that would concentrate their souls on God rather than on the physical comforts that the great cities could now provide. By distancing themselves from the creature comforts, the temptations, of a secular life, they became monastic—those who sought one thing and one thing only, a life fixed on God. By immersing themselves in prayer, they set out to sink into the silence of God within them.

In the desert, thousands lived lives of prayer and fasting, contemplation and self-control, whether in small groups or alone. The lifestyle was indeed a kind of martyrdom. Not surprisingly, after long years of sacrifice and immersion in the scriptures, such wisdom figures became spiritual guides and beacons of spirituality to entire generations from the cities who sought their counsel and their spiritual direction.

Integrating the Practice

To this day, we are learning from the Desert Monastics. The truth is that there is a desert inside you and me that is calling us to become our best selves. It's a place of loss or darkness or struggles with life. It's the part that calls you to recognize your spiritual needs and to heal your inner tensions and divisions of the soul. It's a place of intense spiritual renewal and concentration on the important things of life. Then, after you have learned to do without the superfluities of life, released from a dependency on the things of this life, you are ready to reorient yourself to a simpler, fuller, more truly enriching path to wholeness.

But deserts are difficult places to endure. To go through the desert of my life alone leaves me with one of two possibilities: I will succeed and be stronger than I was before I began this journey to God, or I will collapse under the strain of carrying the denser parts of my life alone. Which is exactly where the Desert Monastics teach us a life lesson of great value. Spiritual companionship and a theology of freedom are important not only to our souls but also to our love of life.

When you find spiritual companionship with those wise enough to allow you to be yourself and loving enough to lead you to your better self, it is the spiritual gift of a lifetime. It helps you to see who you are and who you can become. It teaches you that to grow up spiritually is the heart's portal to acceptance of the random twists and turns of life. It teaches you that happiness comes from within you, not from the accumulation of things outside of you.

Spiritual companionship also teaches you that even the spiritual life is not a straight line to God. As the old monastic story teaches, all of life is a learning process, not an exhibition of never-ending pieties. "What do you do in a monastery?" the seeker asked. And the monastic answered, "We fall and we get up, we fall and we get up." No, happiness is not a record of prayers said, or fasts completed, or pious practices completed.

In some eras, God has been presented as a prize to be won by becoming perfect. To the Desert Monastics, however, God is the living force within, calling you to free yourself from the chains that bind you to the world. They warn you to abandon the addictions, the egotism, the need for power and wealth within you. They model life lived to the full—to its spiritual depths—as more than enough.

God, the Desert Monastics taught, is your compass and your magnet, the end toward which you lean with love and labor with confidence. It is God's hand on your back that you feel urging you to freedom of heart. It is God who beckons you on toward the wholeness of yourself. It is God whose life within you is your security at the end. You have come to know the real God now and freed yourself from the lesser things that you have made your gods. Religion is about so much more than "regularity" or public expectations now. It is about that God, present within you, who does not abandon you to your darkness but holds you up as you search for the light that is your destiny.

The deserts of life expose your weaknesses to you. They eliminate the charades you have developed about yourself and require you to face the fact that your life's problems might be more about yourself than about the problems. They give you the gift of self-knowledge and so prepare the ground of humility that is only then really beginning to flower.

Indeed, the deserts of your life—the relationships that collapsed, the goals that were abandoned, the efforts you never made—can leave you in grief over your failures. But they also leave you full of hope. You know now, having fallen down so often yourself, that life is defined by the amount of effort you bring to living it well, not the applause you get for simply showing up.

At the same time, once you've been seared by the heat of the pressures around you, your deserts remind you that you did not die from them. Instead, you survived to face the next heat wave of the soul and so have the strength to grow into the next wave of revelation. You come to realize that you have not failed; instead, you have triumphed over what you once thought were the weaknesses that would squeeze the spiritual life right out of you.

It is this going into yourself to meet the God within, to understand the needs you have, the strengths you are being asked for, that is the center of the spiritual life. It's there that you come to a new vision of the love of God the Creator for the world and your responsibility to go on cocreating this world. Then you have come to realize that perfection is a myth and a sham. Only personal growth and a commitment to the spiritual life are the virtues that come with being human.

Now you know that you have nothing to fear, no date at which you will pass or fail, only the awareness that here in this desert lies your advance to maturity, to holiness, to trust, and to faith. You know now that you have become more than the average do-it-yourself, paint-by-numbers Christian, who keeps the rules, says the prayers, gives the offerings, follows the documents but has yet to seek the One who is also seeking you. Indeed, the monastic is the one who has braved the truth that God is the one thing worth seeking in life. On the other hand, the monastic is also the one who knows that the God we are looking for is within us, is always with us, does not need to be found but is already the beat of our hearts.

Indeed, the deserts of our lives—the relationships that collapsed, the goals that were abandoned, the efforts we never made—can leave us in grief over our failures. But they also leave us full of hope. We know now, having fallen down so often ourselves, that life is defined by the amount of effort we bring to living it well, not about the applause we get for simply showing up.

45

THE BEGINNER'S MIND

On Newness and Possibility

Zen Buddhists teach that the cultivation of the beginner's mind trains a monastic to be open to all of life in a spirit of newness, of openness, and of possibility.

Benedict of Nursia also teaches monastics to realize that the Benedictine Rule is just "a little Rule for beginners," but it is not *shoshin*—the Zen concept for an attitude of openness common to the beginner's mind. In the Benedictine tradition, the Rule is a guide to a mentally healthy, spiritually sound, and God-centered spiritual life meant to shape the seeker's heart to the eternal awareness of the God within. It is also, it seems, a universal sign of the serious spiritual seeker. Nothing of God is ever enough for those who already sense God in their hearts. The spiritual life is always about tasting more of God newly and forever. It is about listening. Forever listening for the sounds that tie us to the presence of God which lies between Life and this one life of ours.

A beginner's mind implies a kind of change in us that is even deeper than the substantial process of metanoia that comes with the regularity and depth of the monastic lifestyle. Metanoia is a steady attempt to advance in each of the levels and values of the monastic life to the point that we become different people than when we entered monastic life. We become more reflective, more humble, more mature and wise and committed to the currents of life that carry us from spiritual adolescence to spiritual maturity.

A beginner's mind, on the other hand, is a constant openness to new possibilities, to kinds of experiences unthought of till this very moment, perhaps, but interesting. It is about being open to possibilities. A beginner's mind is exactly opposite to the approach of people who already have formed opinions on the subject. These are people who know without doubt that guitars don't belong in church services, for instance. They know that mixed marriages are wrong. They know that all the "good" people live in the suburbs, not in worn-down buildings in the center of town. But to close ourselves off from the differences around us is a recipe for dissatisfaction. It cramps the breadth of our lives. It limits us to very narrow perspectives and experiences.

Racists refuse to accept and enjoy the different cultures around them. Sexists deny what it means to allow all human beings the right to be fully human. And as a result, they never venture out into the rest of the happy and flowing world of ideas and possibilities.

Closedness—social, spiritual, or psychological—blocks a lot of happiness and calls that restriction moral, or right, or proper.

But it's not necessary to live within such narrow confines. It's a choice between openness and growth, between openness and equality.

I was a new writer in the Christian tradition and he the artist in residence in our monastery, when Brother Thomas Bezanson, OBlSB, and I spent long hours together discussing the differing effects of the beginner's mind on the arts. On our lives. It is an exciting concept.

The artists of life are those who allow the possibilities of creation to expand our souls, to extend our influence, to lengthen our reach, and to allow our lives to unfold in new and even wiser and holier ways. For Thomas, beginner's mind was the adventure of making new glazes despite the fact that the public collectors had already identified his best pottery, his most exciting new forms of pottery in an ancient tradition.

Monasticism is a strain of spirituality that has served society in all of its various manifestations—Hindu, Kabbalah, Buddhist, Sufi, and Christian—for hundreds, for thousands of years, but not as a business, only as ancient gifts grown out of new challenges. It does not provide any one particular service, but it does exist to do whatever service any of the traditions may need at any given time—liturgical, social, or spiritual. In all of these traditions, monasticism seeks and lives the essence of the Spirit that drives it. It drinks from the deep wells of whatever tradition has spawned it. It dwells in its spirit of contemplation. It stands out not for the work it does but for the quality of presence it is in a world whose values are so much more material than spiritual. It keeps the tradition alive and so touches even the modern soul at its deepest depths. It embraces the new possibilities that time brings in order to communicate the spiritual life that speaks best to the modern life of every era.

Even more exciting is the realization that the less complex monasticism is, the more powerful its impact on a society rife with frills and domes, spires and towers, authoritative documents and memorial shrines. Monasticism is simplicity at its root and peace at its ultimate. It is not here to maintain its old forms or past formats. It's here to stretch the soul of every century to the needs of that particular time and the cries for the spiritual life.

Monasticism, in other words, goes to the heart of society, to all of its life questions, to the answers that shape our multiple journeys into darkness. It leads the soul through the dead ends of life. It examines life in all its shapes and forms. It ponders and parses all the small pieces of life that, looking weathered, have too often been ignored but have no end of wisdom. It follows the questions that change the way a person sees life. It asks without ceasing: Where did we come from? Why were we born? What is the purpose of life? Where are we going? How can we get there?

Christian monasticism, like the contemplative streams of all the various faith communities in the world, has carried its tradition across the centuries, replanting it in every generation, freshening it from era to era, from possibility to possibility. All the facets of Benedictinism have their own histories, their own forms. And yet all of them—Benedictines, Trappists and Cistercians, Carthusians and Camaldolese—live under the Rule of Benedict written in sixth-century Italy. And from the first it grew. Under its own impetus. In pods unconnected but attached in spirit, it flowered for centuries. And it grows even yet on a globe where there are approximately seven thousand male Benedictine monastics and thirteen thousand women's monastics.

Why? Because there are so few things in life that exist only to live and bloom and light the way for many. Whatever the era. Whatever the ancient structures. Always, the grace that comes with new possibilities. Monasticism is over fifteen hundred years old because it refused to shrivel up and die in old tombs. It rose era after era to being new energy to the soul-life of the time.

Integrating the Practice

Many religious communities come and go over the years. But monasticism as a spiritual concept continues to thrive. Individual monasteries, too, like our own founding motherhouse in Bavaria, which has existed since 1035, are still potent presences in a scattered world. Our own ongoing monastic presence in Erie, Pennsylvania, is an example. Very few early civic institutions of the area still exist but the monastery is still very active in public life here. Many things—huge corporations, great dynasties, banks richer than many countries—crumble and die. The difference is that monasteries do not exist to control anything, to compete with anything, to dominate anything, or to outproduce anything. Monasteries exist to enable people on a spiritual journey to live life to the roots.

Monasteries continue on because of the quality of life they embody—simple, stable, spiritually sound. They are proof that life is about more than success, if by success you mean money. And they are about even more than power, if by power you mean control or influence, in the political sense of the word. Real monastics do not live to maintain the "shoulds" of the past. They exist to demonstrate the fact that everything must become newly alive again in every age. If there were ever proof that the good life is life that sustains the spirit but has no interest whatsoever in storing up things in barns or being movers and shakers, it is monasticism.

Life as we know it in our time is all about personal security and independence, prestige and power. Monastics, on the other hand, throw their lives to the wind, at least according to the metrics of the world around them. They form human community with strangers and pledge to take care of one another, however minuscule their ties. Rather than bury their fortunes in the backyard, rather than spend their lives assuring their own security while they wait for death, they do not strive for prestige, they seek no control. Instead, they go from one end of life to the other knowing that enough is enough and the spiritual life is its own treasure. Monastic life is a life of peace, ministry, spiritual depth, and the perpetual newness that calls each of us to start over again, day after day after day.

Then, at the end of their lives, monastics remember again the words with which Benedict of Nursia closed the Rule. Historians tell us that Benedict himself probably founded only fourteen small, autonomous monasteries before he died. But that Rule had already been adopted by other groups and would become the deep roots and strong trunks of monasteries of Benedictine men and women in our own time. It is an awesome reality.

Benedict writes, on the very last page of the Rule, the most profound words ever about so humble a goal, so simple a path, so rich a life: "Are you hastening toward your heavenly home? Then with Christ's help, keep this little Rule that we have written for beginners." Here, one of the founders of the only religious order that has lasted for over fifteen centuries offers the world "this little Rule." He offers no defense of its profundity, no insistence on spiritual extremes or worldwide acceptance. He makes no grandiose promises and advocates no form of heavenly correctness. He just offers a "little Rule," which has been adapted to every major culture on earth. It is a lesson to be learned as we project the quality of our own lives and works into the future.

This religious Rule, whose foundation rests on the twelve pillars of humility, ends with a humility so profound that it turns all the pomp and circumstance of success, wealth, power, and control back on themselves. Instead, it leaves standing those monastics of all the great traditions who are seeking God within themselves, the one relentless sign we have of the relationship between the Creator and creation, between creation and every soul that delves to hear within itself the echo of God.

For those with a beginner's mind, empty of agitation, free from old "shoulds," open to life, not frozen by past assumptions and absolutes, every day is a new day, not simply another day. This day will hold surprise and depth—and new possibilities forever.

Beginners have no fear of new paths or fresh ideas. The beginner simply knows that God is everywhere, in everything, beyond all past frustrations and false assumptions and waiting to bud within us so that we may all go into the future without fear, without despair and desolation.

For those with a beginner's mind, empty of agitation, free from old "shoulds," open to life, not frozen by past assumptions and absolutes, every day is a new day, not simply another day. This day will hold surprise and depth—and new possibilities forever.

46

OBLATES OF ST. BENEDICT

On Extending the Common Enterprise

There have been lay members of the Benedictine Order since its earliest development. Laypeople, clergy, and non-Catholics may all become oblates of St. Benedict and devote themselves to living out the basic values of Benedictine life without becoming vowed monastics.

Three ways of life are recognized by the Canon Law of the Catholic Church as authentically spiritual lifestyles or vocations:

The first is as ordained diocesan priests under the authority of a local bishop or as vowed religious of a canonically recognized celibate community. These priests and religious devote themselves to parish service or works for the poor.

The second is as those who commit themselves entirely to marriage and family life. They serve one another with love and contribute to the upbuilding of loving communities around them.

The third is as single people in the world devoted to prayer and good works. Those who follow this vocation are free to serve others in ways either priests or religious who are bound to specific works or lifestyles as witnesses to the Gospel life may not be. Or to put it another way, we are, each and all, responsible for living out our lives doing good, some in one form, some in another.

The difficulty with all of these ways of life is that doing anything alone and without support only doubles the effort and often dampens the impact. Even for those for whom solitude and silence are balms, the lack of spiritual companionship is a loss. There's no one to talk to about what I know or what I want to know or at least what someone else knows that I ought to know. There is no one to walk the path with, no one to bring light to my darkness.

This is where oblates come in. Oblates are laypeople who attach themselves to a Benedictine monastery and its spirituality so that they do not tire on the way or lose heart. Oblates form lay Benedictine communities that do not live together but do seek the same spiritual star, follow the same path, and live the spirit of the same Rule, whatever the contour of their particular lives. Guided by the spiritual and communal life of the monastery to which they are attached, they grow in the Benedictine tradition and give new life each to the other. The community carries the oblates along liturgically, spiritually, and as lay members of the Order. The oblates bring new questions, new concerns, and new life into the community. Most of all, they take the community's life and tradition to places and projects where the monastics themselves would seldom, if ever, be. Together we stretch one another into new life.

In fact, Benedictine oblates were the earliest lay members of Benedictine communities in the Church. *Oblate* or *oblation* means offering. Most of the first oblates, the Rule is clear, were children of wealthy families who were "offered" to the monastery in gratitude to God for the families' many gifts. In those early periods, which the Rule alludes to in places, the children of the monastery joined in the community work and development.

Some stayed for life; some left after their years of formation—
much as we would leave a boarding school when we graduated.

But all of them were formed in the array of Benedictine values
which by the ninth century were the ground on which a great portion of Europe found its spiritual identity. Because of this Rule,
generations were formed in community, their land harvested,
their education shared with the peasants, whose lives had been
totally upended with the fall of the Roman Empire.

After all, Benedictine spirituality is a communal spirituality.
It's about the kind of world we create together, whatever the century. It's about what we do for the rest of the world as we build our
own. It is our answer to Jesus' challenge to go out two by two and
do good. Being an oblate, offering oneself as a lay member of a
vowed community in order to go where vowed monastics do not
go—to the bedsides of the dying, perhaps, or the cells of pris-
oners, maybe, or civic projects to build new hospices for the
homeless—extends the spirit of the Rule in both directions.

Integrating the Practice

Oblates of St. Benedict take the Rule and the concerns of the
community beyond the monastery to the neighborhoods and
places where no visitors come. But the monasteries also take their
oblates in and connect them to the monastic community at large.
Then the oblates, along with the community itself, may refresh
their energy at the head of the stream. Then community and oblates together can stretch their understanding of why we all need
to do more in this time of pathological individualism so that we
are really building the "communitarian" world we like to talk
about.

The ancients are clear: There is a common bond between conscious carriers of the great spiritual traditions and seekers of that

same kind of spiritual life in every age that is necessary and empowering for both. In fact, all the ancient Orders—Franciscans and Dominicans as well as Benedictines—developed lay associations early in their history of religious life in the Church. All these orders exist to this day, along with the lay associates connected to most of the apostolic religious orders now as well.

These communities—both vowed Benedictines and committed oblates—need one another. True companions make possible the growth of each other, after all. The real questions for oblates are simple but essential: Why do you exist as an oblate? Who are you in this great Benedictine story? What must you do for the charism to thrive?

Lay religious, by whatever name they've had through time—oblates, a Benedictine term; confraters in medieval monasteries; lay preacher tertiaries of thirteenth-century France; Franciscan, Dominican, and Carmelite Third Orders of the later Middle Ages; Jesuit Volunteers or Maryknoll Lay Missioners of today—are all meant to give new life, wider space, new depth to the religious communities whose charisms they model. At the same time, the task of the communities themselves is to converge their gifts with the gifts of the oblates into one great flame so the rest of the world in all their arenas can see it and envision another way to be alive.

Benedictine life is not a life of rules to be counted and kept; it is a life of values and reflection. It seeks every day to become better at actively listening to others so that you can grow. It concentrates on developing an awareness of the presence of God so that you keep your goals straight. It opens its doors to the world in its commitment to hospitality so that racism and sexism and national chauvinism do not limit the insights of your life. It is devoted to making community out of strangers. It brings dignity to work and respect for workers. It stewards the land and the globe. It seeks peace and justice for the forgotten and despised. It brings stability and responsibility and moderation in all things. Most of all, it devotes itself to the cultivation of these monastic values everywhere, so that, as the Rule says, "in all things God may be glorified."

Benedictine oblates, like the monastic communities from which they come, dedicate their lives to those values. Then— monastics and oblates together—they cast their seeds into the wind and, holding one another up as they go, beget a brand-new way for the world to grow. As the old farmer said, "I turn my back to the wind and cast my seeds about me. It takes no courage to cast my seeds, but it does take courage to go on facing the wind."

Benedictine monastics and Benedictine oblates (OBlSB) make the singular search for a deeply spiritual life a common enterprise, a community gift to many, a companionship. In our separate ways we differ, but, thanks to this melding of lay and religious, we gain from one another the courage that leads us all beyond ourselves.

We are, each and all, responsible for living out our lives doing good, some in one form of life, some in another.

47

PURITY OF HEART

On a Life Worth Living

Among the Desert Monastics, who lived an ascetic life in
the arid lands of Egypt and Syria, the cultivation of a heart
centered on God alone was the essence and the compass
of the spiritual life. They were, as Jesus says, "Israelites
in whom there is no guile."

The Desert Monastics built their spirituality on two major
ideas: the practice of the presence of God and a commitment to purity of heart. Total concentration on the one thing
necessary—a heart centered on the will and love of God—
determined every action of their lives. Purity of heart, this commitment to the consciousness of God, was the laser beam of the
monastic life. It constituted the operational center, the energy,
and the rudder of their lives.

In the world controlled by Rome, where Christianity had become as much a sign of civil identity as a mark of sanctity, purity
of heart was one of the virtues most sought by the Desert Monastics. It marked the spiritual difference between being simply citi-
zens of Christianized Rome and devoting one's entire life to
seeking God.

The Desert Monastics became a countersign to civil religion. Purity of heart—their single-minded attention to the will and presence of God—allayed the spiritual disease of apathy. The listlessness that the Desert Monastics called acedia, spiritual fatigue, the demon of the noonday sun, smothers our love of life. When we stop giving ourselves to anything worth doing, when we slog through life without a sense of direction, of intention, we eat and breathe but we do little to improve the life of the world or strengthen its spine. Purity of heart, on the other hand, is the sense of purpose that keeps us committed to doing the will of God. Once we set our sights on something that makes life worth living, the Desert Monastics knew, all of life changes. We now exist to make our existence count, and this newly found sense of purpose makes boredom—acedia—impossible.

I watched an elderly wood-carver, for instance, on the streets of Rome make a wooden statue of Pinocchio. The man's back was bent and his big flat fingers were thick with calluses. Judging from the looks of his hands, he was now finishing off, at the very least, his thousandth puppet. He had to be tired of scraping them out of square wood blocks again and again. But he leaned over the figure with a tiny piece of sandpaper and rubbed till the wood shone like glass. He was doing what God created him to do—being an artist—and no amount of this work was ever going to tire him out. There was no acedia whatsoever in that old man despite all his years of doing the same thing time after time. This was his mission.

Being committed to something keeps life expanding for us, even when we think that there's nowhere else for it to go. Purpose gives us a sense of importance, of wanting to do even more, even better the next time, no matter how many things we've done already. Finally, a sense of purpose, of resolve, makes getting up every morning worthwhile, win or lose. It is the undaunted determination to do what must be done, however long it takes, whether we get it finished or not. For the Desert Monastic, the purpose was to continue an unending search for God.

Integrating the Practice

How is it possible to find anything in this life that lasts? Well, it depends on where you're expecting to find it. If you're looking at the mechanics of life—the systems at the center of the modern world—the answer is, it's not possible. Functions and processes everywhere change in design over and over again. What's more, the way you do things changes. But if you are looking at the heart, at what people do because it must be done for themselves to be whole, you will easily identify people with purpose.

Our Sister Jerome was ninety-four when she fell in the kitchen and broke her hip. But as they carried her out and into the ambulance she called back to the kitchen staff, "Listen, just leave those tea towels there. I'll finish folding them as soon as I get back." She never got back to that work, of course, but that spirit, that purity of heart, that centeredness, that downright honest sense of purpose is with us still.

No doubt about it: Total concentration on the one thing necessary—a heart centered on the will and love of God—determines every action of your life. It will carry you through life as much as life carries you—only with more fulfillment. It is a beacon from the desert calling you yet to continue your own pursuit of the presence of God, to concentrate always on the purity of heart that seeks one thing only and always.

Your heart is the real compass of your life. The Desert Monastics knew that over fifteen hundred years ago and you know it yet:

Purity of heart is the gift that guides you, leads you, shepherds you from one end of life to the other, always content knowing that you have done what you were born to do. What else could possibly be worth a life?

Every human being, you and I, too, comes bearing a gift meant to be used to do the works of God for the people of the world. But we live in a culture that teaches us we ought to quit as soon as possible and do nothing except relax, retire, and coast through life.

Monastics have been trained to know how necessary and life-giving they are every step along the way to the final work of the will of God. The Rule is clear: "Let everyone, including the sick and the elderly, be given a task in the monastery. . . ." I was sixteen when I heard that for the first time. I thought, Why couldn't they just do what they wanted to do? Then, I got older and learned something about the Desert Monastics and purity of heart and the nature of community, and I figured out the answer for myself. Why give old people something to do? Because they're important, that's why. Because we all need one another for something, that's why. Because we don't just use people till their engines run down and cast them aside for a younger model.

It is a life lesson. Yes, our tasks will change from time to time, but someone will always need us, if only to fold those towels every day after lunch.

May you thank God that you're needed and that what you have to give you have not wavered in giving. May you rethink and renew your purity of heart at every stage of life. May you never find yourself bored and alone, useless and forgotten. May you never forget the presence of God. May purity of heart, the alignment of your heart with the heart of God, carry you through life to its very end. And then beyond.

Purity of heart is the sense of purpose that keeps us committed to doing the will of God: whatever it is, wherever we are. Once we set our sights on something that makes life worth living, the Desert Monastics knew, all of life changes. We now exist to make our existence count; and, this newly found sense of purpose makes boredom—acedia—impossible.

48

MARIAN HYMNS

On Mary, Model Woman

Most celebrated of all the Church music are the four seasonal anthems that mark the place and role of Mary in the development of the faith and theology.

Charles Kingsley, British clergyman and professor of history at Cambridge, made a connection between beauty and the spiritual life that may explain both the import and the impact of Church music. He wrote: "Never lose an opportunity of seeing anything that is beautiful, for beauty is God's handwriting." If beauty is indeed God's handwriting, the relationship between Church music and the role of music in the development of the soul is a clear one.

More than that, however, is the fact that Marian hymns, the four major seasonal anthems to Mary of Nazareth—Mother of Jesus, Mother of the Church—end the Divine Office at Vespers every day of the year. The very placement of the hymns is a comment and a commentary on the place of women in the Church. The hymns themselves are the finest examples of the power of plaiting melody, text, and chant to fulsome and meaningful theology. They are, at the same time, public statements of the value of women in the eyes of God in a church that both sings their value and keeps them invisible at all times, in all aspects of the official Church. Women are the holy secret of the Catholic Church—important to its ministries, ignored in its functions, left out of the development of its theology, denied identity in its sacramental life.

The role and place of Mary, the Mother of Jesus, is a real one, however. Mary, but no other woman, is recognized as part and parcel of the soul of the Church. In fact, Mary is a determinative dimension of the spiritual life. The place of Mary in their lives, as well as average Christians' understanding of the development of the Church itself, is for many the tie that binds. Not theological dissertation, but their human identity with Mary, Mother of the Church, is the part of the Church that is humanized for them. It is Mary who models commitment, courage, and compassion. It is Mary to whom most Christians look for confirmation of their lives and for the support they need to go on in dark times.

It's important, then, that these Marian hymns guide the yearly liturgical journey of the Church. It is through these hymns that its women and young girls, who search so desperately for their identity in the Church, learn the values upon which both their own worth and the faith rest. Otherwise, what proof is there in the documents or liturgy of the Church itself that women have any value at all? Instead of little or nothing official on that subject, there are four major Marian hymns.

The first Marian hymn, from the eleventh century—"Alma Redemptoris Mater," Loving Mother of the Redeemer—is sung from Advent through the Feast of the Purification (also known as Candlemas Day), on February 2. This feast marks the angel Gabriel's announcement of Mary's divine motherhood. Becoming a mother is a time of great joy—and great anxiety as well—for women. Mary's motherhood elevates a woman's existence to the very heart of God. Motherhood, the essence of creation, is the proof that God the Mother is with us all in darkness and in joy. Most of all, this feast, defined in the eleventh century, cites Mary the Mother, whose motherhood has been difficult in so many ways, as a sign of trust in God and promise to many in our own times.

The second Marian hymn, from the fifteenth century—"Ave Regina Caelorum," Hail Queen of Heaven—is sung from February 3 until the Easter Vigil. Mary, we learn here, is not secondary; she is the Queen of Heaven. God clearly recognizes and exalts the gifts and strength of women—and so must we. Mary of Nazareth, as woman, is the portal to a new view of the world and the door to a new world for women.

The third Marian hymn, from the seventeenth century— "Regina Caeli," Queen of Heaven—is sung from Easter Eve until the Saturday after Pentecost fifty days later. We sing here of Jesus' triumph over death; the liberation from sorrow; the fresh new life that leads us beyond suffering, beyond despair. We call on Mary the Mother to intercede for us. After all, this is Mary, Queen of Heaven, who will be silent no more because Jesus came to free us all.

And the fourth Marian hymn, from the twelfth century— "Salve Regina," Hail Queen—is sung from the day after Pentecost Sunday until the Saturday before Advent begins. It is the celebration of the fullness of life, of Mary, Mother of Mercy, whose strength and faith have shaped our own. In this hymn, written in the thirteenth century, Mary is seen as advocate, the one who understands us, whose concerns are not the rules—whatever they are—but us and our needs. It is our pain, our weakness, our need for support that is welcome at this Marian shrine and in this Marian anthem. This is Mary the compassionate one, who does not take sides.

In summary, it is what Mary did to bear Jesus, to raise him, to sustain him in the face of his enemies that brings Jesus to fulfillment and will sustain us as well.

Integrating the Practice

There is an important question before us now; in fact, in this day and age the question is imperative: If Mary is so central a figure to the faith, what does that have to do with women in the Church today and their exclusion from Church ministries? Answer: Everything.

Like the rest of our lives, Mary's life encompasses joy, satisfaction, sorrow, and fulfillment. It is the story of a woman's life and, because of it, the proof of God's recognition of all women everywhere. No matter what the current social or ecclesiastical powers understand or preach. Whether bishops and politicians and male standards everywhere realize it or not, women are chosen by God to bring Jesus into the world and the world into God's embrace. No doubt about it; God will vindicate this truth soon.

Over and over again the community sings these simple Marian hymns. For all our lives we sing them. Then music becomes the memory of our theology. It becomes the beauty of what the soul knows to be true of us, of women. It becomes the tradition of the Church, the truth we teach whether we will allow it to be realized among us in flesh and blood or not. It is about putting the role of women at the center of the Church.

An everlasting hymnody and chant lay out the map of Marian time for us until we know that what started with God was regularly recognized at the core of the Church, in the people, through all the Church seasons.

Even if it is not admitted in print, certainly in the heart of the Church Marian theology has been sung unceasingly, so the world would hear it, generation after generation. As a result, far too many centuries were aware of God's exaltation of women for us to assume that the ideas behind it are fads that came with the twentieth century.

At the end of the day, at the last note of the year, we know that we have gone one more time through the real power of tradition. We are singing forward the value of women to the listening heart of the whole Church. We go on living our own faith lives through the memories we have of learning to love Mary—her strength, her compassion, her sense of justice and mercy—as children and even now.

We develop here, too, a theology of Mary—and women everywhere—whose commitment took her from Nazareth to the upper room, as an apostle among the apostles waiting for Jesus to lead them on. Mary's presence there is always a sign, always a symbol of a woman's concerns, a woman's justice, of the need for the Church to make real its own concern for women and its recognition of its need for the justice and wisdom of women.

Finally, the Marian hymns keep women, their courage and strength, their compassion and mercy, in full light. While male theology and the male Church ignore a woman's place in the economy of salvation, the seasons of the soul, marked by hymnody and chant, reignite that truth in all of us.

Sing on, dear friends. Let no one dampen the chords that ring in every woman's heart.

Like the rest of our lives, Mary's life encompasses joy, satisfaction, sorrow, and fulfillment. It is the story of a woman's life and, because of it, proof of God's recognition of all women everywhere. No matter what the current social or ecclesiastical

powers understand or preach. Whether bishops and politi-cians and male standards everywhere realize it or not, women are chosen by God to bring Jesus into the world and the world into God's embrace. No doubt about it; God will vindicate this truth soon.

49

GOOD ZEAL

On Ardor for Holiness

The truly holy person knows that religion is a double-edged
sword. When it enriches the soul and demonstrates
the two fundamental religious principles—love God and
love your neighbor—the world is better for its influence.
When it is a force meant to satisfy the needs of religious
leaders to control their adherents, religion becomes
cultic and a danger to society.

This small chapter in the Rule of Benedict makes all the difference between monasticism and religious conquest of any ilk.

If there is anything that confirms the authenticity of the Rule
of Benedict, it is chapter 72 of a seventy-three-chapter document.
His last word before closing the Rule is the chapter "The Good
Zeal of Monastics." After pages of concern for prayer, work, hospitality to others, mutual obedience as a staple of community life,
and the familial quality of the community itself, Benedict makes
a statement that seals the nature of monastic life. He writes, "Just
as there is a wicked zeal of bitterness which separates from God
and leads to hell, so there is a good zeal which separates from evil
and leads to God and everlasting life." It's a simple statement, but
it separates good religion from bad religion.

Zeal, you see, is a strange word. When it's used in everyday English, it means fervor—enthusiasm. But the word *zeal* entered the English language in the early fourteenth century, a period of intense religious warfare. Then *zeal* had two completely different meanings, the second of which is often extreme or fanatical as to a religious movement. The distinction is an important one. Of all the feelings common to religious passion, it's zeal that most divides the holy from the unholy. Which means, as Benedict, the founder of the oldest strain of communal monasticism in the Western world, implies, there is such a thing as excess, which spoils religion. But the distinction between good zeal and fanaticism is clear:

Good zeal leads us to love more, to hurt less, to defend the defenseless, to bring justice to populations that are being oppressed, to love the God who created and loves us all. *All* of us. No exceptions. The good zeal of monastics includes caring for the stranger, listening to the needs of one another, immersing themselves in prayer and reflection, caring for the earth, and saving the planet. It also means choosing common sense over extremism when, as the Rule says, the choice is to "pray in the fields" rather than risk lives in order to get back to the monastery in time for community prayer.

Fanaticism is self-aggrandizement posing as holiness by living the incidentals of religious devotion to the ultimate. Instead of fasting for a day, fanatics fast for a month, until weakness makes it impossible to actually live a really holy life. Or they set out to shame those whose morals they disapprove of. Like those religious groups who condemn alcoholics to starvation on Skid Row rather than accept alcoholism as a disease and get them help. Or condemn women sex workers for prostituting themselves to get the kind of money no other job will pay a woman.

Integrating the Practice

Fanaticism pours ignominy and disdain on those who cannot keep up with the physical expectations of asceticism or the extremes of virtue. Worse, fanaticism demands the kind of false obedience that specious religious leadership requires as proof of commitment to themselves. Then the obedience of free will which God requires of us is turned into spiritual immaturity, and though it may not have evil intentions, it is never fully adult.

The fact is that fanaticism, excessive passion even for the good, has done as much harm in the world as it has done good. Fanaticism drove the Crusades. Fanaticism drove the Reformations. Fanaticism drove the Wars of Religion. Fanaticism is pseudo religion to an extreme. Fanaticism is Jim Jones, whose hundreds of disciples in Jonestown, Guyana, followed him to mass suicide in 1978. There is a point at which religion itself can become evil. But no part of evil—for any cause whatsoever—is holy.

The test of good zeal is a simple one: It is goodness after goodness so that life can be good for everyone because you have been here. It is Jesus ministering to the masses who were abandoned and rejected by the holiest professional figures of the Temple.

The reality of evil zeal is clearly with us still. It is evident in the religious types of our own time who reject gay and transgender people. The presence of God is as open to them as it is to anyone else, but instead they get labeled disordered by so-called religious figures around them. It is demonstrated by the Church's attitude toward girls who want to be priests but are disdained for believing that God might want them to follow Jesus, too. It's clear in religion that makes men God and women their servants.

Holiness, on the other hand, is a religious founder reminding his followers before he dies that religion can be as bad as anything else in life—unless we are following religion in all its beneficence in order to become good ourselves. In these words we find hope, possibility, goodness, and God.

Benedict writes: "This, then, is the good zeal which members must foster with fervent love: 'They should each try to be the first to show respect to the other (Rom 12:10),' supporting with the greatest patience one another's weaknesses of body or behavior, and earnestly competing in obedience to one another. No one is to pursue what s/he judges better for herself/himself, but instead, what s/he judges better for someone else. Among themselves they show the pure love of sisters/brothers; to God, reverent love; to their Prioress/Abbot, unfeigned and humble love. Let them prefer nothing whatever to Christ, and may Christ bring us all together to everlasting life."

And that is what this whole book has been about: good zeal, not evil.

The test of good zeal is a simple one: It is goodness after goodness so that life can be good for everyone because we have been here. It is Jesus ministering to the masses who were abandoned and rejected by the holiest professional figures of the Temple.

50

THE MAKING OF THE MONASTIC HEART

On Developing the Heart of God

Truth is about a great deal more than facts, more than the rules a system requires, more than the practices and rituals, oaths and membership obligations it touts. Truth is the integration, the synthesis, of Spirit, soul, heart, and behavior.

Clearly, behaviors may be sound—charitable, truthful, traditional—but the spirit that drives them may be severe and therefore humanly destructive. In the interest of being charitable, we may give people what we want them to have rather than what they need. In the name of truth, we may teach the wrath of an unforgiving God. In the task of keeping the tradition, we can stop the growth of an institution.

A good many spiritual movements across the ages have been found guilty of demeaning, even degrading the very people who sought their spiritual salvation and denying them the fullness of their human development. At the same time, behaviors demanded of a people in the name of religion may be simple, compelling, even very thin on theology but so life-giving, so motivated by a spirit of commitment, so strong that the flaming fire of holiness never dies out. Jesus said, "Come, follow me . . ." and the world changed.

It is the Spirit that leads us on. It is the nature of the Spirit behind it that gives a movement life. It is the Spirit that carries us beyond the burdens of the day, even beyond our own darkness of soul, our own uncertainty of either direction or end, our own dry and waning hope for new energy in a time of drift.

When all is said and done, it's not monasteries—it's not a system of brick-and-mortar abbeys, male or female—that have made a lasting impact on the life of the world. It is the spirit of monasticism that the world recognizes as humanly sound and spiritually healthy—a refuge from institutionalism and a call to personal spiritual depth—when the world is most confused and least healthy. It is the spirit of monasticism that has been the rudder of the Western world. It is the spirit of monasticism that calls us beyond all the systems of the world to find the best of our spiritual selves, to be lights in the darkness of a world struggling to find again the best of its human self.

It is the spirit of monasticism that not only keeps it alive but keeps it changing changelessly.

Monasticism is driven by the spirit of tradition. It preserves and relishes the ancient history of its life. It reverences the saints of its past, their practices and personal strengths, to buttress its own. It lives in the shadow of its overarching sense of changeless change, the understanding that a living spirit protects the fundamentals of its history and finds there the wisdom it takes to change a present practice in order to protect a tradition. Monasticism does not live in the past. It makes the past what energizes both its present and its future.

Monasticism is driven by the spirit of community. The heart of the monastic community is intent on bringing the world around it to a common embrace, to genuine openness, and to a truth beyond the truth of the moment. It's from that perspective that monastics seek guidance from others, respect and guard the dignity of others, seek and share the wisdom of others, listen to one another's needs, and work together to bring the community to wholeness. It's out of that recognition of the goodness of life that the monastics bless all the dimensions of the human condition so that, more positive than negative, the human community grows together in increasing happiness and genuine understanding.

Monasticism is driven by the spirit of reflection. Monastics live in a commonwealth of Gospel, personal pondering, and search for the presence and will of God for the world. For them, every problem prods the questions of why and what and how to do something that will bring the difficult dimensions of life under the domain of goodness and love. Monasticism is a way of life that rests on the consideration of life as it is and life as the will of God wants it to be, the fullness of life for all life, for all peoples, at all times. It is the contemplation of what, having created us, God wants us to do at this particular moment to complete the creation God began.

Monasticism is driven by the spirit of personal growth and development. The function of the spiritual life is not the debasement of people under the guise of false humility. On the contrary. The more developed the individual monastics, the more developed the community itself. Then together the community may venture into the concerns of humanity as a whole, prepared to be a contributing participant in solving the major questions of the time—climate change, political change, social change, personal growth. Then, monastics everywhere with clear minds and great love can be part of moving the issues of the day forward so that neither personal bias nor willful ignorance of the world's concerns leads them into compliance with the demons of the day.

Monasticism is driven by the spirit of service. Monastery doors are open to everyone only when the monastic heart is open as well. Withdrawal from the needs of people in the name of monasticism is not a monastic virtue; it is a monastic guise that gives the lie to the search for one thing only. This search requires that we also search for what we ourselves must do to make the presence of God real in our times. It is our service to one another and the world that changes life—for better or for worse—for everyone we touch.

Monasticism is driven by the spirit of transcendence. The spirit of transcendence is the awareness that life on this earth is meant to be heaven all the way to heaven. It is the ability to remember that the clay of this world is our first step on the way to its afterlife resolution. It is the clear and firm consciousness that this is not all of life, but only the beginning of coming to see that the face of God, the touch of God, the will of God, and the presence of God already surround us, prod us on, call us to the rest of ourselves, to all of creation, to life at its best—both here and hereafter.

All of our lives are spent not from "then to now" but from "now to then." It is the monastic spirit of tradition, community, reflection, growth, service, and transcendence that moves us day after day, all our lives, on the way to the fullness of all of them.

May your own heart be touched by this monastic spirit so that you, too, may both know its fullness and—as have so many thousands over the years—pass it on. Again.

Acknowledgments

The birth of a book is always an interesting process. Some books are a response to high levels of commitment to a subject on the part of the author. Some come out of unusual experiences—like having survived on an uninhabited island, perhaps. Some, like this one, came out of what looked like a casual conversation. The only thing unusual about that is that the conversation at issue took place twenty-five years ago.

It was a slow day. Lunchtime. Mary Lou, the poet friend I'd always called "my muse," was spinning possible programs and publications for next year's calendar. And then she stopped suddenly and said, "You know, what you should do is turn monastic language into language people can understand in their own lives." And I said, "What?!"

"Well," she said, "you tell people how important monasticism is but they don't really know what we're talking about or how to do it themselves. You should do that."

"Mary Lou," I said, "that would take volumes to do." She looked at me, skeptically.

"I'd have to take every monastic concept there is," I went on, "and translate each of them to lay life in the twentieth century."

And she said, "So?"

They were putting water glasses and cutlery on the table. "All right," I said, and gave a big sigh. "What will the chapters be about?" And we started the list: bells, candles, lectio, Divine Office, psalms, work. . . . By the time lunch came, we had twenty-five words that exposed the inner life of the monastic heart. Those words were a launching pad for this book. Then I folded up the menu on the back of which I'd been listing the terms and put it into my folder. It was 1996. Nearly twenty-five years later, last January, I took the list out. And Mary Lou and I sat down together again and added twenty-five more terms as if there had been no time whatsoever between the first conversation and this second one.

It's that kind of slow simmering, quiet thinking, and deep reflection that I'm grateful to have in my life from the Benedictine sisters around me. It makes every word genuine, solemnly felt, and spiritually rooted.

I'm grateful, too, for Keren Baltzer, our editorial director at Convergent, who asked a simple question over morning coffee one day, "What are you working on now, Joan?" And when I explained the genesis of this book—as I just told all of you—I saw the look of interest, of possibility, of uncertainty, of freshness in her eyes. That's the kind of editor every writer needs: one who looks both skeptical about a new idea and lovingly critical about its value.

I'm grateful for the entire editorial team at Penguin Random House, who assessed the idea and found it a good end for a lifetime of monastic ruminations. Most of all, I'm grateful for my manuscript editor, Ashley Hong, who poured her life, her time, and her gentle but clear efforts into clarifying and organizing the fifty topics of this text.

Most of all, I'm grateful for my own staff—Kathleen Schatzberg, who reads with a red pencil and a great heart. I'm forever grateful for Susan Doubet, OSB, who works over my shoulder on

every draft of the work—giving advice, watching for complexities, staying with the editorial process to the very end of the last
sentence. And, finally, I'm grateful for the community that raised
me and held me up through all this searching and stretching of
one of the oldest traditions of Western religious life, Benedictine
monasticism.

And, oh yes, to Mary Lou Kownacki, OSB, who had the tenacity to spend twenty-five years convincing me that this was a
book crying out to be written.

Obviously, I am a writer blessed with friends, with resources,
with a great professional team, and with years of excellence to lean
on in one of the best publishers any writer has ever known.

I am, in fact, just as grateful for my readers who allow me to
pursue contemporary spirituality with their sincerity and insights
in mind.

ABOUT THE AUTHOR

JOAN CHITTISTER has been writing serious pieces of personal reflection since she was fourteen years old. A woman of many interests—music, swimming, study, research, and journalism chief among them—the one central and ongoing commitment of her life has always been writing. Called out of a freshman classroom to explain to the nun-teacher she had for English whether some adult had helped her write her first high school essay, the conversation ended with an abrupt direction: "If you really wrote every bit of this essay yourself, Joan, report to J-room, the journalism office, immediately after school." As Joan puts it, "After that first night, I never left J-room again."

That conversation has taken Joan Chittister from editor of a high school newspaper to a would-be short-story writer, to the author of more than fifty books, in English and eleven languages around the world. All of them written in the course of a life immersed in administration as well.

Joan entered the Benedictine Sisters of Erie in 1952 and, after a stint of teaching in parochial schools, became Prioress of her own Benedictine community in Erie, Pennsylvania, president of the Benedictine Federation of St. Scholastica, president of the Leadership Conference of Women Religious, and a founding member of the Global Peace Initiative of Women, a UN partnership organization that has traveled the world creating a chain of both governmental and public action groups everywhere.

As a result, these grassroots connections and person-to-person conferences on global justice, universal peace, and the equality of women have led Joan to speak to audiences in over sixty countries and territories around the world.

She received her BA from Mercyhurst University in Erie, her master's from the University of Notre Dame, and her doctorate in speech communication theory from Penn State University in 1971. Joan was an elected Fellow of St. Edmunds College, Cambridge University, England.

Joan lives with her community at Mount St. Benedict Monastery and with a very small parrot by the name of Lady Hildegarde—Lady, for short.

ABOUT THE TYPE

This book was set in Garamond, a typeface originally designed by the Parisian type cutter Claude Garamond (c. 1500–61). This version of Garamond was modeled on a 1592 specimen sheet from the Egenolff-Berner foundry, which was produced from types assumed to have been brought to Frankfurt by the punch cutter Jacques Sabon (c. 1520–80).

Claude Garamond's distinguished romans and italics first appeared in *Opera Ciceronis* in 1543–44. The Garamond types are clear, open, and elegant.